Trivial Pursuit ™

GENUS™ EDITION
Quiz book
‖ ∙ PARRAGON ∙ ‖

GENUS EDITION

First published in Great Britain in 1993 by Boxtree Limited.
Questions © 1993 Horn Abbot International Ltd.
Trivial Pursuit is a Registered Trademark of
Horn Abbot International Ltd.

Horn Abbot International Ltd., Villa Franca,
Hastings, Christchurch, Barbados, West Indies.

1 3 5 7 9 10 8 6 4 2

Designed and typeset by Swann, Pearce, Jeanes Ltd.
Printed and bound in Portugal, by Printer Portuguesa for
Parragon Book Services Limited.

A CIP catalogue entry for this book is available from
the British Library.

ISBN 0-75251-187-4

Photographs courtesy of the
Hulton Deutsch Picture Library,
Syndication International,
Scope Features, NME and Channel 4.

Trivial Pursuit™

· C O N T E N T S ·

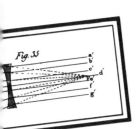

Trivial Pursuit ™

Q: What is the connection between the Queen and Frank Bruno?

Trivial Pursuit has probably generated more arguments than any other board game in history. During my eight years as question compiler I have been called the 'Most Hated Man in Britain', and have received a letter from one player whose wife left him because of his obsession with the game.

■ So why did such a simple question-and-answer game take the world by storm?

■ Her Majesty the Queen is a known addict, and Frank Bruno once told me that he enjoys the game ('Know what I mean, Brian?'). In other words, the questions are aimed at everyone, not just the specialist or intellectual.

■ Before using a question I make sure that it fulfils at least one of the following criteria:

■ Is the answer there at the back of everyone's mind so that, even if they can't remember it, they will say, 'Oh yes!' as soon as they hear it?

■ If the question is difficult will people find the answer informative and is there at least one clue in the question?

■ If the question is so trivial that hardly anyone can guess the answer, will it at least give them·a laugh?

■ My own favourite question is *What did the first dog to be fitted with contact lenses fail to see?* The answer is, of course, *the car that ran it over*.

■ And yes, I do occasionally get things wrong, but a question is only as good as its source material. A top-selling encyclopaedia currently lists Pluto as the most distant planet from the sun whilst any schoolboy will tell you that intersecting orbits mean this honour goes to the planet Neptune.

■ Now that **Trivial Pursuit** is available in book form the fast, furious fun and fighting can spill over from the after-diner table to trains and boats and planes. Maybe the Queen will install a copy in her throne room and Big Frank might have a quick read between rounds.

■ Enjoy it, it's only trivia.

Brian Highley.
U.K. Trivial Pursuit compiler.

1

G Which is the world's most populous Portuguese speaking city?

E What names did Walt Disney choose when he animated the seven small characters below?

H How many Earp brothers showed up at the O.K. Corral?

AL Which literary classic is set in the fictional community of Avonlea?

SN What illness caused 20 British hospitals to cancel all routine admissions in December 1989?

SL Why do a steeplechaser's spiked shoes have a special pattern of holes in them?

2

G Which neighbouring country do Russians call Khitai?

E What was Cliff Richard's 1990 Christmas number 1?

H What name was given to the military arm of the Viet Minh?

AL Which two of the four Gospel writers were Apostles?

SN Do pigs suffer from sunburn?

SL How many people are in each boat in a rowing coxed pair race?

3

G What was the name of the world's first National Park?

E What were you watching if Penny Junor told Matthew Collins where to go?

H Which year saw the creation of the United Nations?

AL Who, in 1983, became the first British novelist to win the Nobel Prize for literature since Winston Churchill?

SN What is the common name for insects belonging to the genus *Apis*?

SL What two values can an ace have in a game of pontoon?

4

G Which country is sometimes referred to as Montezuma's Realm?

E What song did Ferry Aid take to number one for the Zeebrugge ferry disaster?

H What type of French missile sank two British ships during the Falklands fracas?

AL What chess piece does Alice start out as in *Through the Looking Glass*?

SN What term for a collapsed star was coined in 1967 by Professor J. A. Wheeler?

SL Which popular vodka cocktail was so named because oilmen stirred it with their tools?

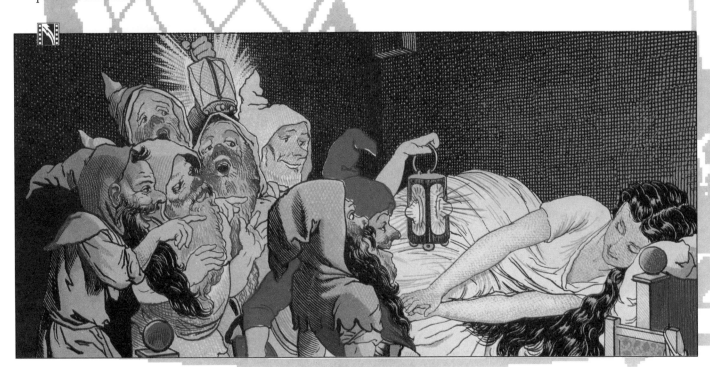

5

G How many blue triangles are there on the Union Jack?

E Which pop star said "When I dress up, I think, Oh God, what will they think down in Watford"?

H Which country was ruled by Akbar in the 16th century?

AL Which University did Tom Brown go to after his schooldays?

SN What is the common name for the rockpool creature *asteroidea*?

SL Which video game took its name from the Japanese work "paku" meaning "to eat"?

6

G Which ocean would you paddle in if you were holidaying in Zanzibar?

E Which John Lennon song was Britain's first ever posthumous Christmas number 1?

H Which country's 1983 free elections brought Raul Alfonsin to power as president?

AL Whose book *Tall Tales* tells of a relationship with Mick Jagger?

SN Do tarantulas spin webs?

SL What sporting activity was this actor famous for?

7

G Which canal flows through the Mira Flores and Gatun locks?

E What did Ronald Reagan just have removed in the 1941 film *King's Row* when he said: "Where's the rest of me"?

H Which city left its Industrial Promotion Centre standing as a monument to its bombing?

AL Which bit of a newt goes into the witches' brew in *Macbeth*?

SN Which was the first completely Asian country to have a satellite in orbit?

SL What three colours are striped across the top of a bottle of Italian *Galliano* liqueur?

8

G How many great Pyramids does Giza boast?

E Which successful 1979 film saw the authorities trying to cover up a possible nuclear disaster?

H What benefit was first introduced to Britain on 1st January 1909?

AL What is draped over the branch of a tree in Salvador Dali's painting *The Persistence of Memory*?

SN What six-letter word is another term for pure china clay?

SL Which Australian was the first cricketer to score 2000 runs and take 200 wickets in test matches?

9

G Which sprawling American state boasts the most airports?

E Who always rings twice according to the title of a 1982 Jessica Lange & Jack Nicholson movie?

H How did President Banda manage to warrant a twenty thousand pound parking fine in 1985?

AL What does Mr Stapleton collect as a hobby in *The Hound of the Baskervilles*?

SN What is the fundamental unit of heredity?

SL What, at Maplins Holiday camp, was 50 metres by 22.8 metres if it really was Olympic size?

10

G What is the name of Australia's most famous inselberg?

E Which of *Disney's* Seven Dwarves is first alphabetically?

H Where did Mathias Rust make his most famous 1987 landing?

AL Whose kidnapping started the Trojan Wars?

SN What is the British name for the animal on which the Americans based their *Teenage Mutant Ninja Turtles*?

SL Which card, in a normal pack of playing cards, is known as the death card to occultists?

11

G Which country boasts almost half of the world's telephones?

E Which 1939 Robert Donat film was remade in 1969 as a musical starring Peter O'Toole and Petula Clarke?

H What was the *Mayflower's* cargo on its second trip to America?

AL Which two Biblical locations were notoriously known as "The Cities of the Plain"?

SN For what do silviculturists grow and care?

SL Which female tennis star said: "If you're small, you better be a winner"?

12

G Which state is the home of Australia's heavily exported *XXXX* lager?

E Which early morning TV star made a feature of bashing young children on the head with a big foam-rubber object?

H Who was called 'The man of destiny'?

AL What instrument are there two of in a string quartet?

SN What does a polythelian stripper have at least three of?

SL Why was the 1957 RAC Rally cancelled?

13

G What are dried in Kentish Oast Houses?

E Whose first single not to make it to number one was called *I'm The One*?

H Was Cynthia Payne found to be guilty, or not guilty, of controlling prostitutes in her Streatham home?

AL What is the world's most popular production from the Children's Television Workshop?

SN What powered the trains through New York's first subway when it opened in 1904?

SL Where were the 1936 Summer Olympics held?

14

G Which is the only US city to be named after a British prime minister?

E Which Beatles' song was a top 40 hit for Ella Fitzgerald?

H What previously banned product did America's three main TV channels agree to advertise from February 1987?

AL What kind of stone was the stone in *Romancing the Stone*?

SN What kind of bird was traditionally used to test for gas in coal mines?

SL Which head of state opened the 1976 Montreal Olympics?

15

G Which range of hills is central to the Northumberland National Park?

E Which song was an R & B number one hit for Big Mama Thornton before Elvis had even recorded it?

H What did Cecil Rhodes believe you had to be, to win first prize in the lottery of life?

AL To whom was Beethoven's *Eroica Symphony* originally dedicated, when written in 1804?

SN How many of the major planets are smaller than earth?

SL Which famous American is said to have invented water-skiing?

16

G Which American motor manufacturer was named after the founder of the city of Detroit?

E Who did Leander visit when making nightly swims across the Hellespont?

H What anniversary did the Royal Mail celebrate in 1985?

AL Which famous story series features a bird called a Roc who could lift an elephant?

SN Of which heavenly body did *Ranger 7* provide the first close-up photographs, on 15th July 1965?

SL How many prizes are there on the *Bullseye* prize board?

17

G What ancient tourist attraction is seen at its best between Corbridge and Vincolanda?

E What title did bandleader Harry Robinson adopt when fronting his Eleven on such hits as *Hoots Mon*?

H Which British political party was said to have been launched on a diet of claret and chips?

AL What stops the train in Agatha Christie's *Murder on the Orient Express*?

SN What natural feature appears in fault, block, folded and dome varieties?

SL Who was the captain of Brazil when they lifted the World Cup for the third time?

18

G Which is America's 'Golden State'?

E Who was Cilla Black's co-host for the first series of *Surprise Surprise*?

H Who did Arthur Scargill endorse in the 1988 fight for the Labour leadership?

AL Which famous composer was Franz Liszt's son-in-law?

SN What did 16th-century gourmets refer to as a 'Peruvian Apple'?

SL Where is the Barbarians rugby club ground and club house?

19

G Which canal links the Atlantic to the Pacific?

E Who are the only band ever to have made a debut appearance as bill-toppers in front of 120,000 people in Hyde Park?

H Which open space in London did Oliver Cromwell sell for seventeen thousand pounds in 1652?

AL Which Biblical character was 'the voice of one crying in the wilderness'?

SN Which blood group flows through the veins of universal donors?

SL Who did Steve Ryder succeed as presenter of *Sports Night*, know what I mean?

20

G Which country boasts the most miles of railway lines?

E Which 60s pop star sang the *Whatever Happened to the Likely Lads*? theme song?

H How many years of World War II saw official bread rationing in Britain?

AL What was the title of *Six Days of the Condor* changed to when it was filmed?

SN How many humps does a newborn camel have?

SL Over which course is the Cesarewitch run?

21

G How many cents are there in a quarter?

E From which US statesman did 'Hawkeye' Pierce of *M*A*S*H** take his first two names?

H What is France famous for that was originally called 'the Louisette'?

AL How old was Adrian Mole when he began writing his diary?

SN What does DOS mean to a computer operator?

SL How did goalkeeper Frank Swift die?

22

G How many cents are there in a dime?

E Who owned Grantley Manor immediately prior to Richard De Vere?

H How many British General Elections has the Liberal Party won?

AL How many wheels does Constable's *Hay Wain* have?

SN What name has the Warner Brothers Animation Department given to the flightless cuckoo?

SL What did Denis Compton wear on his head according to a major 1950s advertising campaign?

23

G What is the central focus of attention in the main pilgrimage square at Mecca?

E Who played Lytton in *Lytton's Diary*?

H Which part of Mussolini's anatomy was damaged when the Hon. Violet Gibson shot him?

AL What are you out to shoot if your bullets have been specially made from the metal of a silver crucifix?

SN For which childhood disease did Dr. John Enders develop the first successful vaccine, in 1962?

SL Who, in 1990, became the youngest ever World Snooker champion?

24

G Which island do Australians call 'A little bit of England'?

E Who were the most famous residents of the planet Skaro?

H Which group of islands were officially at war with the Netherlands from 1651 to 1986?

AL Who is the first person to be born in the Bible?

SN As what is the foot complaint 'pernio' better known as?

SL What eight words precede the sporting couplet "His hands can't hit what his eyes can't see"?

25

G What is the name of this mountain and where can it be found?

E Which TV sidekick rode Scout?

H What vote did Margaret Thatcher lose by 738 to 319 in 1985?

AL How many books in the Bible refer to Eve taking a bite from an apple?

SN Which bird used to be called the laverock?

SL In which country was cricket's Ted Dexter born?

26

G Which European city calls itself 'Little Paris'?

E Which TV detective appeared in his opening credits with a halo over his head?

H Who was the first woman to lead a British trade union?

AL What name was given to Billy Fisher in the title of the novel in which he was the main character?

SN What do the letters V.T.O.L. mean to a pilot?

SL From what are snooker balls made?

27

G Which Austrian city boasts Mozart's birthplace?

E What was the name of Dr. Cameron's house?

H Who won the 1983 Nobel Peace Prize and was then told he couldn't go to collect it?

AL Which Dickens novel is subtitled *Or the Parish Boy's Progress*?

SN What is 'pogonophobia' the fear of, which would cause sufferers to avoid Noel Edmonds, Clement Freud and billy goats?

SL What tournament offers a trophy with the inscription "The Gentleman's Single-Handed Championship of the World"?

28

G Which country's largest lake is called Lake Eyre?

E Which future star played Rodney Harrington in *Peyton Place*?

H What natural disaster struck York Minster soon after David Jenkins had been consecrated there as Bishop of Durham?

AL Which great composer had the first names Johann Sebastian?

SN Why is a *Boeing 747* always heavier at take-off than at landing?

SL Which newspaper claimed Clive Lloyd as a reader?

29

G Which Egyptian city boasts the Karnak Temple?

E What regular programme did the BBC introduce with the theme music *Girls in Grey*?

H What happened to Lady Jawara, the President of Gambia's wife, when he was at Prince Charles' wedding?

AL How many Sherlock Holmes books include the famous line: "Elementary, my dear Watson"?

SN What peculiar feature of the green ghost would make someone suffering from 'blennophobia' unsuitable as a *Ghostbuster*?

SL How many consecutive strikes are required for a 'perfect game' of ten pin bowls?

30

G Which river falls over Niagara Falls?

E What was detective Andy Crawford's father-in-law called?

H What nine words followed Norman Tebbit's statement: "My father didn't riot"?

AL How did Van Gogh kill himself?

SN What did the Wright brothers appropriately call their plane?

SL Who broke Bruce Jenner's decathlon record in 1980?

31

G Which popular group of holiday isles were once known as the 'Fortunate Islands'?

E This horror actor was buried in the cape he'd worn when playing the role of Count Dracula. What was his name?

H What are Dorsetmen Loveless, Loveless, Hammett, Standfield and Brine collectively remembered as?

AL Which controversial author won the 1981 Booker Prize with *Midnight's Children*?

SN What is measured in Curies?

SL Which pop duo joined the snooker players on the hit song *Snooker Loopy*?

32

G Which is the most distant country from New Zealand?

E For which organisation did *The Champions* work?

H Which Thames pleasure cruiser sank with the loss of 57 lives in 1989?

AL Which country's folk music includes the manic depressive 'fado'?

SN How many manned flights to the moon have there been?

SL What is Scotland's only Group-One racecourse?

G Which country's motto is *In God We Trust*?

E Which male took to wearing blue dresses after being Margaret Thatcher's *Spitting Image* speaking voice?

H Which company was charged with corporate manslaughter following the Zeebrugge ferry disaster?

AL Which jazz singer made her first Proms appearance in 1990 as the speaking voice of God?

SN How many degrees separate the Equator from the North Pole?

SL Which club first got together at the Star and Garter Coffee House in Pall Mall in 1750?

G Which country has IL as its international car registration letters?

E Which actress gave birth to Rosemary's Baby in the film of that name?

H Which city was badly damaged in 1989 by the second-worst earthquake in America?

AL Which famous operatic singer's surname translates into English as 'Blackhead'?

SN What do 'gynophobics' fear?

SL What do the letters I.P.A. stand for, on a can of beer?

G What colour triangle indicates a Youth Hostel on an Ordnance Survey Map?

E What year finally saw an end to compulsory afternoon pub closure in England?

H Which London store was bombed during the 1983 Christmas shopping rush?

AL Which popular opera is based on a play by David Belasco?

SN What is the maximum possible total number of solar and lunar eclipses in one year?

SL What did the Eastern bloc call their games in 1984 when they all did a big moody and dropped out of the Olympics?

G Which city's cable cars were America's first mobile National Monument?

E Which US president advertised *Chesterfield* cigarettes?

H Which former Italian Prime Minister's requiem mass was one of the last public appearances of Pope Paul VI?

AL Which Richard Strauss opera includes a collision between a skier and a toboggan?

SN What is the term for a single bacteria?

SL Who were Argentina playing against in the 1966 World cup when their captain Rattin was sent off?

G Which country paints *S.N.C.F.* on the side of its trains?

E Which televison beer expert shares his name with a pop singer?

H Which is the only year this century to have seen three different Popes?

AL Which Olympic rowing gold medal winner is more famous for his baby books?

SN What would you ask a man to stick out if you wanted to have a good look at his septum?

SL Which football club has been in Divisions 1,2,3,4 and in the old North and South Divisions 3?

G As what are the residents of the island of Lesbos known?

E Who was the first Canadian comedian to record his own TV series for the BBC?

H What did 1 in 5 of the world's population watch happening on their televison sets at 1.47pm GMT on 20th July, 1969?

AL What piece of American sporting equipment is covered with poems in *Catcher in the Rye*?

SN How many eyes does a vampire bat have?

SL What new code regarding women's hats was introduced to Ascot's Royal enclosure in 1984?

G In which Australian state is the city of Sydney situated?

E Which soap are you appearing on if you drink in *The Swan*?

H What did America's 1920 Volstead Act prevent the manufacture of?

AL Which novel did *W. H. Smith* remove from sale following complaints in January 1989?

SN Who owned the private zoo where two keepers were killed by tigers in 1980?

SL How many times did Stirling Moss win the World championship?

G Of which country is the island of Corsica a region?

E Who became famous via *Neighbours* but once worked in a video rental shop?

H Which European country's monarchy was restored in 1975?

AL Who said that English was taught "so bloody badly" that his own staff couldn't spell or write properly?

SN Which country's wines were first discovered to contain Glycol anti-freeze in 1985?

SL Which boxer was known as the Manassa Mauler?

41

G What reached London in 1665 with catastrophic results?

E Which Beatles' song gave Candy Flip their first major hit?

H What was the full name of this famous British explorer?

AL Who went into hiding following Moslem condemnation of his *Satanic Verses*?

SN What unusual feat can you perform if you have scotopic vision?

SL Who announced his retirement in 1988 but still managed to hammer Frank Bruno in 1989?

42

G Which city was the setting for *Boys From The Black Stuff*?

E Who was lead singer with the Commotions?

H What century saw Joan of Arc beatified as a Saint?

AL Which leading painter of soup cans died in 1987?

SN What type of fruit includes a variety known as 'brown turkey'?

SL Which snooker player was fined ten thousand pounds after failing a 1988 drugs test?

43

G What major U.S. tourist attraction's nearest town is Kissimee?

E Which entertainment and information service was first established at Savoy Hill, London in 1922?

H Which political party banned 20 of its young members from attending their own conference in 1988 in case they embarrased the party?

AL Which London museum houses the country's biggest collection of decorative arts?

SN To what did the name of America's 'General Purpose Vehicle' get reduced?

SL How many athletes did Germany send to the 1948 London Olympics?

44

G Which English county is famous for its rare Blue Vinny cheese?

E Which foreign former actor received an honorary knighthood in 1989?

H What did a February 1988 majority of 54 vote to allow into the House of Commons?

AL What new style of art did Picasso introduce with his painting *Les Demoiselles d'Avignon*?

SN Why did Marie Curie name one of her radioactive discoveries Polonium?

SL Who upset Hitler's ideology of a 'Master Race' at the 1936 Olympics?

45

G Which Palace can be seen from Winston Churchill's grave in Bladon?

E Which Hollywood comedy star was charged with rape and murder in 1920?

H What was Britain's first airline called in an attempt to shore up the power of the Empire?

AL What new style of art did Perol Freres exhibit at the Paris Exhibition of 1900?

SN What was the most distant planet to be photographed by *Voyager 2*?

SL Which football ground saw the tragic deaths of many Liverpool fans during the 1989 FA Cup semi-final?

46

G Which country would you visit to see the Palace of the Moguls?

E Who wrote *Lady Be Good*?

H Who read Edward VIII's abdication speech?

AL What was the Labour Party's official newspaper called until it folded one week in 1987?

SN Which famous bridge builder designed this railway station, and where can it be found?

SL Which fruit can be found in a Black Forest Gateau?

47

G What would a Japanese tourist mean if you bumped into him at the races and he said: "Fuku"?

E Who presented television's *That's Show Business* quiz?

H What variation on *Hail to the Chief* was chanted outside the White House when Richard Nixon resigned?

AL Which museum would you visit to see the Portland Vase?

SN What could 60% of the British population no longer get on the National Health Service from April Fools Day 1989?

SL How many kilograms does the bar weigh before any weightlifting weights are added to it?

48

G Which are the four European countries whose names begin with L?

E Which film starring a then-unknown had enough punch to win the 1976 best picture Oscar?

H Which American general said: "The army is the Indian's best friend"?

AL Which museum would you visit to look at *Whistler's Mother*?

SN Which former chemist made the final speech at the 1989 International Conference on the Ozone Layer?

SL Which spirit gives a Singapore Sling its kick?

49

G Which former Portuguese colony has Luanda as its capital?

E Which song flew up the charts for Norman Greenbaum and for Doctor and the Medics?

H Which country was code-named *Wildflower* by its World War II allies?

AL Which Canadian coined the phrase 'Global Village'?

SN Of what does 96 per cent of a cucumber consist?

SL What animal's head is pictured on a Gordon's gin label?

50

G Which country's national anthem is *Jana Gana Mana*?

E What month gave Eric Clapton an album title?

H What sort of missiles made headlines when they arrived at Greenham Common in November 1983?

AL Which magazine did Canadian novelist Hugh McLennan call: "The *Kraft* cheese of literature"?

SN Which multi-millionaire flew around the world in a record four days in 1938?

SL What kind of sauce blankets Eggs Benedict?

51

G What island are you on if you are visiting East Malaysia?

E Which pop singer's London flat was the scene of two deaths in 1986?

H Which US president's father wired him: "Don't buy one more vote than necessary. I'll be damned if I'll pay for a landslide"?

AL Which E. M. Forster novel took a rise in the ratings when it became the subject for a 1985 David Lean film?

SN Which scientist gave his name to the Farad — an electrical unit of capacitance?

SL What are washed, scraped and bearded before they become *moules mariniere*?

52

G Which language, other than English, appears on the photo page of a British passport?

E Who played Dick Tracy in the 1990 film of that name?

H Which country's King Henry IV once promised "a chicken in every pot"?

AL What was sold for $1.8 million to Germany's Gutenberg Museum in 1978?

SN What are listed in the periodic table?

SL Which sea can you see from the first tee at St. Andrews?

53

G Which country's notorious drunks hold up their glasses and shout: "Za vasheh"?

E Which of *Disney's* Seven Dwarves is last alphabetically?

H What deadline date of 1991 was Iraq given to get out of Kuwait?

AL What modern word would replace the word "wherefore" in the line "Wherefore art thou, Romeo"?

SN What gives off the active smell in smelling salts?

SL What is the main ingredient in an Indian dish of dahl?

54

G Which main street connects Piccadilly Circus with Oxford Circus?

E Which Yorkshire town shares its name with the prison where Robert Redford got himself locked up in *Brubaker*?

H What was inserted between the 0 and 1 of Outer London telephone numbers in 1990?

AL What two animals appear in Picasso's painting *Guernica*?

SN What kind of fuel powers a 'gas' cigarette lighter?

SL What colour wine is squeezed from Chardonnay grapes?

55

G Which country is known as Azania by many of its natives?

E What year saw the release of James Dean's *Rebel Without A Cause* and *East of Eden*?

H How many days were lost when Britain adopted the Gregorian Calendar in 1752?

AL Which best-selling book runs to 1,189 chapters?

SN How many minutes does it take for a standard L.P. to make 100 revolutions?

SL What sort of craft was Florida's Joe Kittinger the first to pilot across the Atlantic, in 1984?

56

G Which of the following is a genuine Norwegian town — Lowerbelch, Middelfart, Upperpuke or Underwee?

E Which 1959 film featured the character Jimmy Porter as a market stall holder?

H What sacred pets made the noise that warned Rome of the Gaul's attack in 390BC?

AL Which pianist is said to have coined the expression "I cry all the way to the bank"?

SN Which animal is formally known as *Ursus Maritimus*?

SL Which former England football captain and manager died on his 76th birthday in 1990?

57

G Which British city gave its name to the Australian city originally called Coal River Settlement?

E Which 9-fingered pop pianist starred in the film *It's All Happening*?

H Who was head of the Gestapo?

AL Who didn't attend Richard Burton's funeral at the request of his widow?

SN What are pushed up by the process of orogeny?

SL Which crooner's son won the 1982 United States Amateur Golf Championship?

58

G Which motorway would you use if the Queen Mother wanted a lift on the back of your tandem from London to Windsor?

E Which country made Hendrik a national hero because of a story in which he stuck his finger in a hole?

H Which English port did Napoleon set sail from to his exile on St. Helena?

AL What type of hat did this famous detective wear?

SN How many letters of the alphabet are used as Roman numerals?

SL What high achievement was Junko Tabei the first woman to reach?

59

G Which engineer's statue has its back to you if you're looking out of the window of the Paddington Station bar?

E Who died in 1988 after painting probably the most famous portrait of the Queen?

H Which Henry was the first Tudor monarch?

AL What year first saw the Queen's portrait age, on a five pound note?

SN What does the sun convert into helium?

SL Which British football club was involved in the Heysel Stadium disaster?

60

G What form of transport did China report a two year waiting list for in 1983?

E What was the Bionic Woman's name?

H Which '60s scandal was the basis for the film *Scandal*?

AL Who is Aaron's lover in *Titus Andronicus*?

SN What does the 'Jesus Bug' do to earn its name?

SL What does Steve Davis do when he wants to screw?

61

G What would the letters I.Y.H.F. mean to a hitch-hiking student?

E Whose worst enemy is called Scunner Campbell?

H Which years saw both Wilson and Heath as Britain's Prime Minister?

AL How many years lapse between the presentations of the Oberammergau Passion Play?

SN Would a giraffe have been able to swim back to Noah if it had fallen off the Ark?

SL Who had a bad fall during the 1839 Grand National and still has his name mentioned every time the race is run?

62

G What colour are official New York taxi cabs?

E What was the biblical name of the dog rescued by Benny in *Crossroads*?

H How many Pope Fabians have there been?

AL Which northern holiday resort occurs as a surname in Dickens' *Hard Times*?

SN What covering did Frederick Walton make from a combination of linseed oil, gums and ground cork?

SL What sport features in Paul Simon's song *Night Game*?

63

G Which Australian city was named after William IV's wife?

E Who was the brother if Suzanne Crough was the sister and Shirley Jones was the mother?

H How many British prime ministers have been assassinated (up to and including January 1993)?

AL Which gallery would have to give you permission if you wanted to produce *Hay-Wain* T-shirts?

SN What Peruvian word is given to seabird droppings used as fertilizer?

SL Which team won the FA Cup in 1939 and kept it for the seven years during the war?

64

G Which is America's only state capital that includes the name of the state in its own name?

E What day would it be tomorrow if the day before yesterday was the day when *Tomorrow's World* was screened before it moved to Tuesday?

H Who is the only Englishman to have been both a knight and a saint?

AL Which book follows someone's progress towards the 'celestial city'?

SN What measurement was originally defined as one 10-millionth of the distance from the Equator to the Pole?

SL Who did Stephen Hendry beat in the 1990 final to become World Snooker champion?

65

G Which is the 'Lone Star State'?

E Which gambler won the 'Dragon Club'?

H Who said: "I never, repeat never, met her" of a woman to whom he'd given two thousand pounds?

AL Which major composer had the first names George Frideric?

SN What is measured with a gravimeter?

SL What piece of indoor sporting equipment is Louis XIV known to have installed at Versailles?

66

G Which is a Siberian river — Tom, Dick or Harry?

E What was the surname of Hoss, Adam and Little Joe?

H Who likened wholesale privatization to "selling the family silver"?

AL How many times is the word 'corn' used in the Bible?

SN What is the minimum number of metals required to produce an alloy?

SL What do you do in basketball that is the equivalent of a football kick-off?

67

G Which city is known as the 'Daughter of Rome'?

E What was the Boswell's dog called on *Bread*?

H Who was made to apologise by the Queen after throwing paint at a group of American photographers?

AL Which building would you visit to see the tomb of Charles Dickens?

SN What substance is nicknamed 'Texas Tea'?

SL In which sport did Australian Betty Wilson make headlines during the 1950s?

68

G Which Italian city's main tourist attraction is almost always hidden and was proved to be a fake in 1988?

E Which four-letter radio station was run by 'The Big Guy'?

H Who had walked on the carpet that was cut up and sold with signed certificates from bishops in 1982?

AL Who became Poet Laureate in 1984?

SN Which Swiss psychoanalyst identified a collective as well as a personal unconscious in the human psyche?

SL How many hoops should there be on a croquet lawn?

(69)

G Which river flows through Rome?

E What are the first names of 'The Brothers McGregor'?

H Who, in 1980, described Ronnie Reagan's economic plan as 'Voodoo economics'?

AL In what language is the Prince of Wales' two-word motto always written?

SN What is the zodiacal sign for Taurus?

SL What do the sporting ladies of Osiris and Blondie do?

(70)

G Which is England's oldest New Town?

E What two words got you gonged on *Take Your Pick*?

H What was the average age of American troops in the Vietnam War?

AL Which literary creature used the name Saunders whilst living in the forest?

SN What is an acephalous person lacking?

SL Who is this famous boxer and on which BBC1 sports quiz did he used to captain a team?

(71)

G Which mountainous country's highest mountain is the Grossglockner?

E Which musical town was the setting for the musical *Dreamgirls*?

H What event in 1980 became Britain's longest ever newsflash?

AL Which piece of music by Khachaturian was a top hit for Love Sculpture?

SN Of what is a dactylogram an impression?

SL What was unique about the positions of the two captains in the 1934 World Cup final between Italy and Uruguay?

(72)

G What do 100 Greek leptas make?

E Which punk manager had a King's Road boutique called *Sex*?

H Who was Oliver North's secretary?

AL What occasion would you be attending if you joined in the singing of a threnody?

SN Which is the only planet with a clockwise rotation?

SL What first did Enriqueta Basilio achieve at the 1968 Olympics?

G What is the Chinese equivalent of Japanese 'otemoto'?

E What was the name of the space craft in *2001:A Space Odyssey*?

H What name was given to modern Cambodian leader Saloth Sar?

AL Which composer married Anna Magdalena?

SN Where would you have to stick your finger if you wanted to touch your vomer?

SL How often are Davis Cup competitions held?

G Which southwestern city is the home of the National Lifeboat Museum?

E What topped the British TV ratings at Christmas every year from 1979 to 1989?

H Who was the flamboyant leader of Canada's Liberal Party?

AL What are the four German spies doing with each other when Richard Hannay secretly watches them in *The 39 Steps*?

SN How many inches of rain fall on the moon's Sea of Showers in the average April?

SL Who, at the 1984 Olympics, said: "This is the best moment of my life since my granny caught her tit in the mangle"?

G Which is Japan's largest island?

E What is Britain's longest-running television soap series?

H How many days did the *Six-Day War* last?

AL What sport is the subject of almost a complete chapter in *Tom Brown's Schooldays*

SN What is the more common name for the pain known as 'otalgia'?

SL How many days after filling in her application was Zola Budd lucky enough to gain British Citizenship?

G Which is the largest city on the African continent?

E Which children's series' cast released an anti-drugs record called *Just Say No*?

H Which university city gave its name to the trousers that provided 1922's male fashion rage?

AL From which magazine did Sonia Sutcliffe originally win a record six hundred thousand pounds in damages?

SN Why did Canadian Customs refuse entry to a bracelet, sent by Brigitte Bardot, to raise funds for baby seals?

SL Which stadium is scheduled to host the 1994 World Cup final?

G To which saint is Westminster Abbey dedicated?

E What *EastEnders* role did Susan Tully fill when she stopped being Suzanne in *Grange Hill*?

H What is the tragic link between Queen Astrid of the Belgians and Princess Grace of Monaco?

AL Which Edinburgh railway station is named after one of Sir Walter Scott's novels?

SN What two words describe a drug used to disguise the use of another drug, such as steroids?

SL What horse did Pat Taffee win the Cheltenham Gold Cup on in 1964-65 and 66?

G What colour is the Golden Gate Bridge?

E Which *EastEnders* pub burnt down?

H Which American president signed the Treaty of Versailles at the end of World War I?

AL Who wrote the book *Upwardly Mobile* which was described by one court as 'grossly defamatory'?

SN What does L.C.D. stand for in mathematics?

SL In which country did James Hunt have his final Grand Prix win?

G Which city was the setting for *Gangster*?

E Whose puppet clones are all called 'Little Frank'?

H Which Sicilian city was destroyed by an earthquake in 1908?

AL Which British crime fiction writer died four days after Chinese Premier Chou En-Lai?

SN For what did Jonas Salk discover a vaccine in 1952?

SL Who did *Spitting Image* say had run a race in a time which qualified her for a British Passport?

G Which popular European tourist country dishes up a pork and bean stew called 'Feijoada'?

E Which jazz trumpet virtuoso is credited as having invented 'scat' singing?

H Where did the incident take place that was described by a group of MPs as "tantamount to capital punishment without trial"?

AL Which famous dancer's children drowned in the Seine with their nurse?

SN Who rang bells to make dogs dribble?

SL What was the sport of glamorous 'Gorgeous Gussi' Moran?

 81

G Which country's most northerly mainland point is called 'Easter Head'?

E Who was known as 'Empress of the Blues'?

H Who broke the House of Commons' mace during a poll tax debate?

AL Which George Bernard Shaw role was specially written for Mrs Patrick Campbell?

SN Which deaf and blind student graduated from Radcliffe College, USA, in 1904?

SL Who ran a race at Oxford with number 41 on his chest on 6th May 1954?

82

G Which volcano could erupt over into the town of Ottaviano?

E What anniversary did the Royal Television Society celebrate with a visit by the Queen in 1987?

H Which new London airport was opened by the Queen in 1987?

AL Which famous artist died in the same year that Shakespeare was born?

SN What did the Government blame extra high inflation figures on in December 1987?

SL Which British boxer made a winning comeback in January 1991?

83

G Which city was the setting for *Van Der Valk*?

E Which quartet claimed to have shared a joint in the loo at Buckingham Palace?

H Which 87 year old former-nurse was awarded the Freedom of the City of London in 1908?

AL Which sculptor died in a fire at her home in St. Ives?

SN What drug is obtained from this tree?

SL Who 'temporarily retired from British athletics' in 1988 and went back home to South Africa?

84

G Which is the largest of the Channel Islands?

E What is the nearest rival pub to televison's *Flying Horse*?

H Who led the 1918 raid which captured Damascus?

AL Who won an injunction against Norman Tebbit because his book was grossly defamatory?

SN What did Louis Washkansky receive, that someone had had before him, that nobody else had ever had before?

SL Which boxer is known as Black Cloud?

85

G What is the better known name of the Collegiate Church of St. Peter?

E Which TV soap spawned the short-lived spin-off *Damon and Debbie*?

H What was George VI's first official act when he took over as king from his brother Edward?

AL How many stone tablets did Moses bring back down from the mountain?

SN What does the 'F' stand for in the formula F = ma?

SL What is Bulgaria's official national sport?

86

G How many official languages does Switzerland have?

E What was Richard Dimbleby's last state occasion?

H What did Howard Carter have on his top lip when he opened Tutankhamen's coffin?

AL Which ancient London theatre was picketed by actors to prevent bulldozers from covering it over?

SN Why were Haitians linked with homosexuals, haemophiliacs and heroin addicts in 1984 newspaper reports?

SL What sport saw England contest its first Test Match against Australia in 1930, at Wimbledon?

87

G The famous Blue Train runs between this city and another European capital. Name them.

E What is Phillip Schofield's puppet pal called?

H Which civil rights leader won the Nobel Peace Prize in the same year that Nelson Mandela was imprisoned?

AL Which literary detective played cricket for Eton?

SN What does the six-footed *Musca domestica* become when it flies into your home?

SL How old was Bjorn Borg when he retired from professional tennis?

88

G For how many years are Australian prime ministers elected?

E Which children's TV show was first presented in 1952 and was still going strong in 1989?

H Which Vietnamese leader died two days too early to watch ITV's first colour transmission?

AL To what is the French newspaper *L'equipe* entirely devoted ?

SN Which was the third country to launch a satellite into orbit?

SL Which football club seriously considered penning in supporters behind electric fences?

89

G Which country administers Greenland?

E Which comedian did *The Sun* claim had eaten a hamster sandwich?

H Who was the first Pope to attend an Anglican service in Britain?

AL Who kills the heroine in Berg's opera *Lulu*?

SN What is the maximum possible number of solar eclipses in one year?

SL As what are the former British Empire Games now known?

90

G What colour is the cross on the Swiss flag?

E Who became a star of *Coronation Street* after being Wilfred Pickles' pianist on *Have A Go*?

H Which oil rig sank with the loss of 166 lives in 1988?

AL What hobby did composer Dvorak enjoy alongside his pigeon-fancying?

SN What do heliologists study?

SL On which country's currency does this famous cricketer appear?

91

G What is the proper name for the Houses of Parliament?

E What instrument did Rolf Harris play on Kate Bush's *The Dreaming*?

H Who won damages of three hundred thousand pounds after a newspaper claimed she'd had an adulterous affair with Prince Andrew?

AL To what culinary use did Haydn's wife put many of his valuable manuscripts?

SN What does the letter *B* stand for on a camera shutter?

SL What did Antonio Garrido do with his ball to warrant disqualification from the 1986 Madrid Open golf championship?

92

G Which is the only Australian state with no S in its name?

E Which hospital would you visit to meet *The Young Doctors*?

H Which European country was offered to Elizabeth 1 in 1575?

AL Who is famous as a photographer, as an artist and as the designer of the costumes for *My Fair Lady*?

SN What animal is described as 'caprine'?

SL To restrict the spread of which disease was the 1967 RAC Rally cancelled?

93

G What are the names of the two little boys pictured doing unnatural things to a wolf on the badge of Rome?

E Who presents *Catchphrase*?

H What was the fruity surname of Zimbabwe's first president?

AL Which newspaper's very first headline was SECOND SPY IN GCHQ?

SN Which planet has the shortest year?

SL What annual sporting event takes place over a 4 mile 374 yard course?

94

G Which is the only Great Lake with no Canadian shores?

E What is the relationship between Fitz and John according to a TV title?

H Who proved to be absolutely correct when she said: "I'm not interested in a third party. I do not believe it has any future."?

AL Which year saw the Queen's portrait suddenly age on British coins?

SN What is the international radio word for the letter Z?

SL Who got the gold medal when Nancy Hogshead and Carry Steinseifer swam a dead heat in the 1984 Olympic 100m freestyle?

95

G Which city's tourist attractions include the Jorvik Viking Centre?

E What was Vince's daily duty at the Crossroads Motel?

H Of whom, in 1985, did topless model Samantha Fox announce that she was going to become a neighbour?

AL What did *Hitch-Hiker's Guide to the Galaxy* character Zaphod Beeblebrox have two of that most men have to be satisfied with only one?

SN How many bones are there in a human skull if the ears are cut off?

SL What would you be doing if you pegged out after a four ball break?

96

G What is America's 'Mother City of the South'?

E Which TV series centres around the activities of lawyers Brackman, Chaney and Kuzack?

H What did Primate of All Ireland, Cardinal Thomas O'Fiach, say it was okay to join so long as it was only for the social activities?

AL This man is known as 'The Knight of the Sorrowful Countenance.' What is his more common name?

SN With what gas are most modern airships filled?

SL Who won the 1912 Olympic gold medal for football with a score of 19-1?

G Which Italian city boasts that it's 'the home of Parmesan cheese'?

E Which spoof soap had Mrs Overall as the cleaning lady?

H Who told a group of British students that if they stayed in Peking for much longer they'd have "slitty eyes"?

AL Who would you be hanging around waiting for if you had the role of Vladimir in one of Beckett's best known plays?

SN Which vitamin aids blood clotting?

SL Which round saw the end of Ali's fight with Richard Dunn?

G Which Spanish holiday costa is served by Malaga Airport?

E What did Dr Who call 'Bessie'?

H Who was Colonel in Chief of the Royal Marines at the time of Prince Edward's resignation?

AL Which major work of art did Hereford Cathedral put on sale in 1989?

SN What are kept in an arboretum?

SL What was a goalkeeper afraid of, according to the title of a film directed by Wim Wenders?

G Which Syrian city is known as the Pearl of the Desert?

E What was Uhura's job on the *Starship Enterprise*?

H Which year saw the sinking of the *General Belgrano*?

AL Whose only opera was *Fidelio*?

SN What can you waggle if you have well-developed auricularis muscles?

SL What does the term 'King Pair' mean to a cricketer?

G Which country originated Gouda cheese?

E Which TV married couple were played by David Kossoff and Peggy Mount?

H Who did Spain fight in the 1804-1814 Peninsular War?

AL What did Len Deighton's *The Berlin Memorandum* become when it was filmed?

SN To what domestic use are the leaf tips of Camellia sinensis put?

SL What colour flag is raised at firing ranges to indicate that shooting is in progress?

G Who opened the almost immediately criticised M25 with the carp: "I cannot stand those who carp and criticise"?

E What was the name of Wilbur Post's talking horse?

H Which of the Channel Islands is famous for its lack of cars?

AL From which city did Shakespeare's 'Two Gentlemen' come?

SN What is a male giraffe called?

SL What term is used in skittles to describe the knocking down of all the pins, with a ball still left to throw?

G Which American state calls itself 'The Last Frontier'?

E Which soap is set on a built-up corner of Lord Derby's estate?

H How many other countries joined the EEC on the same day as Britain?

AL Who wrote his *Journal of the Plague Year* at the age of five?

SN Which French town's name became famous after the discovery there of prehistoric skeletons in 1868?

SL Which boxer's nickname was *The Ambling Alp*?

G What colour flag indicates an E.E.C. approved clean beach?

E Who was backed by the Yellowcoats on the theme music for *Hi-De-Hi*?

H Which British coin was minted from silver until 1672?

AL What 10th century Bohemian king became a hero at the hands of Victorian hymn-writer J. M. Neale?

SN How many legs does a millipede have on each of its body segments?

SL Which pop star's yacht capsized during the 1985 Fastnet race?

G What do Italians call their motorways?

E Which of the deadly sins is missing — Lust, Pride, Envy, Avarice, Sloth, Gluttony?

H Which member of the Royal Family was christened on December 21st 1984?

AL What nickname did Charles Dickens give to his character John Dawkins?

SN What did a Great Dane called Caliph unfortunately do, whilst on trial for his life for biting?

SL How many home matches did Manchester United play on their way to the 1990 FA Cup Final?

G Which county has an 88 mile footpath called Robin Hood Way?

E Which Ray Charles rocker was an adaptation of the hymn *Jesus Is All the World To Me*?

H Who went on to become an Eastern communist leader after working as a pastry chef at London's Carlton Hotel?

AL Which country is the setting for the ballet *Giselle*?

SN Where would you find the Fissure of Rolando?

SL What is soccer's equivalent of the American football position called 'safety'?

G Which European country's capital stands on the island of Zealand?

E What two-word German greeting brought the response "Nuts you dope" from Fred MacMurray in the 1943 film *Above Suspicion*?

H What was the name of the French line that faced Germany's Siegfried Line?

AL Which Asian city was designed by Sir Edwyn Lutyens as a grand symbol of the British empire?

SN Which animal's breasts go into a 'terrine de canard a l'orange'?

SL For what sport does Clive Everton most famously provide the TV commentary?

107

G Does the Vatican issue its own coins?

E Who did Hayley Mills think the murderer was who she sheltered in her shed in *Whistle Down the Wind*?

H Which crown is placed on an English monarch's head at the moment of coronation?

AL Which novel did Ernest Hemingway say that "all modern American literature comes from"?

SN What facility on a Space Shuttle includes a footrest, hand-grips, seat belt and suction fan?

SL What word does the following spell: dash-dash, dash-dash-dash, dot-dash-dot, dot-dot-dot, dot?

108

G What is the better known name for Rome's Flavian Amphitheatre?

E Which disaster movie included the song *We May Never Love This Way Again*?

H What year saw the 50th anniversary of the Battle of Britain?

AL What did Longfellow declare to be "the universal language of mankind"?

SN Which industrialist hit on the idea for mass production after watching workers in a meat-packing plant?

SL How many times has the Olympic Games been held on the African continent?

G Which country's people were found to be the world's top television viewers in a 1990 survey?

E Who played the Fay Wray role in the 1976 remake of *King Kong*?

H To what did Sir Francis Drake change the name of the boat *The Pelican*?

AL Which popular Verdi opera is based on Dumas' novel *The Lady of the Camelias*?

SN Of what was the fossil archaeopteryx one of the earliest known examples?

SL Which sportsman is told that his balls mustn't weight more than 1.62 ounces each?

110

G What would a Tongan do with his pa'angas?

E Which member of Wings went bankrupt in 1986?

H Which country's flag did Ferdinand Magellan fly when he went on his world cruise?

AL What is the most common two-letter ending of English adverbs?

SN What was the active ingredient in the Victorian sedative called 'laudanum'?

SL Which English cricket captain was given the nickname 'Sardine' in Australia?

111

G Which Middle Eastern city is the home of the Evil Counsel?

E Which was the first rock band to play four consecutive nights at Wembley Stadium?

H What was Rex Hunt governor of, that brought him worldwide headlines in 1982?

AL Which children's writer's books were re-launched in 1990 with absolutely no mention of gollywogs?

SN What do insects do through their spiracles?

SL Who captained Australia in the famous 1960 Tied Test?

G What is the capital of Arizona?

E Which song was a hit for both Elvis Presley and the Pet Shop Boys?

H Which country produced almost all of the world's diamonds until the 18th century?

AL Whose *The Interpretation of Dreams* sold only 351 copies during its first two years in print?

SN How many rows of sprocket holes are there on a 36 exposure roll of *Fuji 200 ASA* film?

SL What size boot is thrown in a welly throwing contest?

(113)

G Which of the following is a real Australian mountain — Tom Price, Tom White, Tom Spright or Tom Kite?

E What group name is used by Chris Lowe and Neil Tennant?

H What was the religion of India's Mogul emperors?

AL Which novel finds Milo Minderbinder elected as mayor of half-a-dozen Italian cities?

SN What was set as the maximum age when the original seven US astronauts were selected?

SL Which swinging swimmer retired in 1929 with 67 records to his credit?

(114)

G What is the capital of Luxembourg?

E Who wanted to go the distance with Apollo Creed?

H Which member of the Royal Family was described as "a kinky devil" by former girlfriend Vicki Hodge?

AL Which novel begins: "The Mole had been working very hard all morning, spring-cleaning his little home"?

SN What, according to Margaret Thatcher, would the government ban from being put into British fridges?

SL Which wrestler complained in 1990 that some airlines made him pay for two seats instead of one?

(115)

G What is Australia's most popular religion?

E Which TV game show ends with the 'Star Spin' round?

H Who was the first explorer to set foot on all continents except Antarctica?

AL Which city would you have been spending your 1505 summer holiday in if you had bumped into Michelangelo and Leonardo da Vinci?

SN Which was the only EEC country to vote against stronger health warnings on cigarette packets in 1989?

SL Which board game's name is said to come from the Welsh for 'little battle'?

(116)

G Which southwestern British town attracts tourists with claims that both King Arthur and Jesus Christ lived there?

E Which year saw the first in-flight movie: 1925, 1935, 1945 or 1955?

H What prize did this man win in 1983?

AL Which great actress continued her career after having a leg amputated?

SN Which city do scientists say would see 23,000 deaths if it suffered an earthquake like the one it suffered in 1906?

SL Who won the 1970, 2000 Guineas on Nijinsky?

117

G Which English county is the home of the lake that Rudyard Kipling was named after?

E What was the verdict in the Fatty Arbuckle murder and rape case?

H How did gay rights protesters reach the floor of the House of Lords in their protest against 'Clause 28'?

AL What nationality was composer Edward Grieg?

SN What year saw the first powered flight in a heavier-than-air machine?

SL Which of Marilyn Monroe's husbands was known as Joltin' Joe?

118

G What name is given to snacks traditionally served on a plate balanced on top of a drink in Spain?

E What was the stage name of William Claude Dunkenfield?

H What year saw the birth of the Commonwealth of Australia?

AL What was the name of Tintin's dog Milou changed to when the story was translated from French into English?

SN What is unusual about this animal's claws?

SL Which Belgian football stadium witnessed 41 deaths when English fans rioted?

119

G On which island did the Dutch build their New Amsterdam?

E Which Phil Collins hit also charted for Jam Tronik?

H What two letters appeared on the very first Girl Guides hats?

AL Which of Viking Penguin's 1989 book releases gained by far the most publicity?

SN What was the name of car enthusiast Count Emil Hellinek's daughter?

SL For what reason did Sir Ranulph Fiennes call off his 1988 walk to the North Pole?

120

G What national park sees the annual Ten Tors Walk?

E At which school did Ken Barlow teach?

H Who was the youngest Conservative candidate in the 1951 General Elections?

AL Where did Prince Charles not wish to see "a monstrous carbuncle on the face of an old and much-loved friend"?

SN How many gallons of water does the average camel's hump hold?

SL How many times did Cambridge win the Boat Race between 1975 and 1991?

121

G Which country played host to the Battle of Waterloo?

E Which soap are you appearing on if you are drinking in *The Jolly Sailor*?

H Which year saw both Hitler and Mussolini leave their 'proper jobs' in favour of politics?

AL Which Spanish surrealist painter died in 1989?

SN What did it become legal for consenting adults to do in their cars after a 1981 Government decision?

SL Who was the second in the World motor racing Championships for the four consecutive years 1955-1958?

122

G Which Underground line was the world's first?

E What is the local paper in Albert Square?

H Which country saw the Mau Mau uprising?

AL Who do the Continental Historical Society of San Francisco claim is the real author of *Alice In Wonderland*?

SN What extinct creature is the basis for *Sesame Street's* Big Bird?

SL Who had won the most Boat Races up to and including 1990?

123

G Which continent boasts the Atlas Mountains?

E What fruit juice turns champagne into a Bellini?

H What occasion in 1977 was celebrated by allowing pubs to stay open all day?

AL What sport features in the play *Outside Edge*?

SN What do sanguisugent creatures crave?

SL Who took a wicket with his first ball after returning to cricket following a 1986 ban?

124

G Which province grows most of Canada's apples?

E Which Howard Hughes war film gave its title to a bikers' fraternity?

H Who lit the first of a chain of 102 beacons on the day before his wedding in July 1981?

AL Which work by Menotti was the first opera written specially for television?

SN What does a bicornate animal have two of?

SL What famous sports complex has changed its address from Worple Road to Somerset Road?

125

G Through how many oceans does the Equator pass?

E What hollows out the log to form a genuine didgeridoo?

H How was St Lawrence, the patron saint of cooks, said to have been martyred?

AL Why did Ravel and Prokofiev have to write special pieces of music for pianist Paul Wittgenstein?

SN What is the better known seven-letter name for acetylsalicylic acid?

SL Which soccer club was fined £105,000 in 1990 for making irregular payments to players?

126

G Which Venezuelan river has the distinction of sharing its name with a Womble?

E To whom does the *Starship Enterprise* belong?

H Which famous conservationist was murdered by Somali bandits?

AL Which female name was used as a title by Gilbert and Sullivan and Tchaikovsky?

SN What kind of storm is a 'haboob'?

SL For what reason were the 1987 Badminton Horse Trials cancelled?

127

G Which country has a Mount Bruce?

E What is the name of the cartoon character who features on the quiz show *Bullseye*?

H Who was the first Chancellor to have his budget televised?

AL From which Shakespeare play did Tom Stoppard borrow his Rosencrantz and Guildenstern?

SN How many layers of skin cover the epidermis?

SL What derogatory term for new military recruits gave its name to a popular game?

128

G Which county would you head for if the Prime Minister invited you round to the official country seat for tea?

E Which children's television signature tune gave the Settlers their only hit?

H Whose first words after being shot were "Honey, I forgot to duck"?

AL How many of the Brontë sisters lived to see their 40th birthdays?

SN What element's chemical symbol is *I* ?

SL Who won the 1952 Olympic 10,000 metres on the same day that his wife, Dana, won the javelin?

129

G Which of the 'Dynamic Duo' shares a name with a town in Turkey?

E What was concealed in Napoleon Solo's pen?

H Which country's exceedingly large king brought his own chair to Prince Charles' wedding?

AL What weapon did Samson employ to slay a thousand Philistines?

SN What colour is a male blackbird?

SL Who owned Classic winner Dunfermline?

130

G Which river flows through Innsbruck?

E Who had a cleaner called Mrs Scrubbit?

H Which 1980s mass-murderer said that he occasionally took a body from under the floorboards to watch TV with him?

AL Who wrote *Bedside Showjumping*?

SN What did ancient Egyptian women do with the metal antimony?

SL Which is England's oldest golf club?

131

G Which African country is famous for Richard Leeky's fossil-rich Olduval Gorge?

E In which series, other than *Dallas*, would you find one of the Ewings?

H How much per head did the Government offer to the staff at GCHQ, in Cheltenham, as a bribe to leave the union?

AL What was the surname of fairy tale writers Jakob and Wilhelm?

SN How many women have landed on the moon?

SL What was this footballer the first to achieve off the football field?

132

G Which is the only English city that begins with the letter T?

E What was led by Major Adams?

H Which government minister turned up at Molesworth Peace Camp wearing a flak jacket?

AL What name is given to a five line poem which might begin: "There was a young girl from Cheshunt"?

SN Which is the morning star if Venus is the evening star?

SL Which city's Olympics were the setting for the film *Walk Don't Run*?

133

G Which is the largest of the United States?

E Which consumer affairs programme had Esther Rantzen and John Pitman as assistants?

H Whose comment on the first moon landing was: "This is the greatest week in the history of the world since the creation"?

AL Why are 'Camel Hair' paintbrushes so called?

SN What method for brewing coffee was invented by James Mason in 1865?

SL Which regular *Private Eye* feature, lists cock-ups by sports commentators?

134

G As what is East Pakistan now known?

E What kind of 'Yarn' was *Murder at Moorstones Manor*?

H What was Timothy Evans given in 1966 after being hanged in 1950?

AL What was the profession of the two ladies in the children's nursery rhyme *Lucy Locket*?

SN Of what does a bicaudal cow have two?

SL Which board game was invented by Alfred Butts?

135

G Which city is the home of the *Fiat* motor company?

E Which TV series was set in London's Eaton Place?

H Which country fought against Japan in the Battle of the Coral Sea?

AL Which 'Lady' was the most famous 'mistress' of Wragley Hall?

SN What, in 1781, became the first new planet to be discovered since ancient times?

SL What sport did Prussia's Baron Gottfried von Cramm play at international level?

136

G What is the name of this structure and for what purpose was it originally built?

E What was the number 3 hit for the Hollies in 1969 and a number 1 for them in 1988?

H Which Ivan was 'Terrible'?

AL Who is the owner of the world's biggest collection of Leonardo da Vinci's drawings?

SN What beverage did Louis Pasteur first pasteurise in 1864?

SL Of what does a poker 'Full House' consist?

137

G Which county attracts tourists to the seaside village of Clovelly?

E What towns from Arkansas and Texas did Harold Lloyd Jenkins combine for his country and western stage name?

H Whose attention drawing gimmicks have included waving a pair of handcuffs around at a Tory party conference?

AL Which TV comedian wrote *Katy and the Nurgla*?

SN Which element has exactly the same name as a planet?

SL What nationality is speedway rider Ole Olsen?

138

G Which county are you in if you're 'On Ilkley Moor bah't 'at'?

E What was this *M*A*S*H* major's nickname?

H Who gave a £1.25 million charity cheque to Bob Geldof in October 1986, that he couldn't have given to him three months later?

AL Which member of the *Dynasty* cast was born near Paddington Station on 23rd May 1933?

SN What game is played on a *Bally 'Captain Fantastic'*?

SL Which year first saw women taking part in Olympic track and field events?

139

G Which South American country produces *Maracaibo* coffee?

E Whose appearance on the same stage as the Monkees was campaigned against by the Daughters of the American Revolution?

H What did Tory MP Keith Best apply for six lots of that he was only legally allowed one lot of?

AL Which actor provided the macabre voice-overs at the end of Michael Jackson's *Thriller* hit single?

SN Of what is a Queen Alexandra Birdwing the world's largest variety?

SL What did Abebe Bikila wear when he won the 1964 Olympic Marathon that he didn't wear when he won the 1960 event?

140

G Which London street is associated with Sweeney Todd?

E Which song has charted twice for Jimmy Young in two different versions?

H Which Belgian port saw the *Herald of Free Enterprise* set sail with its bow doors open in March 1987?

AL How did Vivian of *The Young Ones* get rid of the TV when a licence inspector called?

SN Why does the stonefish warrant a mention in the *Guinness Book of Records*?

SL Who was a Nobel Peace Prize winner, a British M.P. and silver medallist in the 1920 Olympic men's 1500 metres?

141

G Which major New York leisure area was laid out by Fred Olmstead and Calvert Vaux and opened in 1876?

E Which two 'ladies' live in the fictional village of Stackton Trestle?

H What was the *Bounty's* cargo at the time of its most famous mutiny?

AL Which painter threw a knife at Paul Gauguin in the French town of Arles?

SN Which valuable element has the atomic number of 79?

SL Which liqueur is the French equivalent of Curaçao?

142

G Which Asian country is split east to west by the Hindu Kush?

E What is Kris Kristofferson's C. B. handle (code name) in *Convoy*?

H On which aircraft carrier did the Duke of York serve, during the Falklands War?

AL Whose autobiography is titled *First Lady from Plains*?

SN What kind of school for dogs was first established in Nashville, Tennessee, in 1929?

SL What is your sport if you get off on a dock start, a beach start or a scooter start?

143

G What are there three of to every person in Wales, according to a 1990 survey?

E Who said of taxidermy: "The chemicals are the only thing that cost anything"?

H Who captained the *Victory* at the Battle of Trafalgar?

AL What order of columns support the Parthenon in Athens?

SN What was the profession of William Semple, who, in 1869, became the first man to add sugar to chewing gum?

SL Which Englishman bettered his own 1980 Olympic 1500 metres time when he won the race again in 1984?

144

G Which major city is served by Vnukovo and Sheremetyevo airports?

E With what was Audrey Hepburn's doll expensively stuffed, in the movie *Wait Until Dark*?

H Who was America's sixteenth president?

AL Whose pop art comic recreations include *Blam!* and *Whaam*!?

SN Of what two words is the name 'daisy' a corruption?

SL Of what is ancient Pompeii citizen Publius Ostorius known to have survived 51?

145

G Which very, very famous London tourist attraction is marked only with *13 tons, 3cwt, 3qtrs, 15lbs*?

E Which film featured a plot by the People's Front of Judea to kidnap Pilate's wife?

H Which of the King Louis' was the last Bourbon to live at Versailles?

AL Which animal most regularly features in Minoan art?

SN How many bends are there in a standard paper clip?

SL What year will see the centenary of the modern Olympic Games?

146

G What was Port Stanley's name briefly changed to during the Falklands fracas?

E Who played the female tough-talking star in the film *A Fish Called Wanda*?

H Which cosmetics giant began in 1886 as the California Perfume company?

AL What was Shirley Conran's follow-up novel to *Lace*?

SN How is 12.5 per cent expressed as a fraction?

SL What is the round stump on the front of a saddle called?

147

G What is Sri Lanka's main export crop?

E Which company received Prince Edward's resignation in June 1990?

H What did members of the SS have tattooed in their armpits?

AL Whose place at the guillotine was taken by Sidney Carton in a *Tale of Two Cities*?

SN How many times a day should you do it if it is marked 'Q.I.D.'?

SL What is the USA's official folk dance?

148

G Which African country boasts the continent's biggest man-made hole?

E What six words precede "A policeman's lot is not a happy one"?

H How many prime ministers served under Queen Victoria?

AL Who are the two subjects in religious paintings called *Pieta*?

SN What is the name of the nearest G2 Spectrum Yellow Dwarf to the Earth?

SL Which US president took to jogging to enhance his athletic image and them almost collapsed in a road race?

149

G Which is the most famous peak in the Cascade Mountains of the USA's Washington State?

E What was the Elizabethan Blackadder's first name?

H Who were interned when Franklin D. Roosevelt signed Executive Order 9066 on 19th February, 1942?

AL Which novel begins its journey: "My father had a small estate in Nottinghamshire; I was the third of five sons."?

SN What flavour of yoghurt was blamed for a major outbreak of botulism in 1989?

SL How many musical instruments is a woman allowed to accompany her in Olympic floor exercises?

150

G How many times each day should a Moslem point his prayer-mat towards Mecca?

E Which famous actress took up American citizenship in 1941 to show her hate for the Nazis?

H What three-word slogan was printed above the Wembley *Live Aid* stage?

AL Which literary bear was born in 1926?

SN What kind of transport did Auguste Piccard use when he became the first man to reach the stratosphere?

SL Which British football stadium saw 56 deaths in a tragic 1985 fire?

151

G Which canal's biggest lock is at Pedro Miguel?

E What controversial programme on the Gibraltar IRA murders did the Government try to ban?

H Which Irish town's Remembrance Day parade was bombed in 1987?

AL Which annual finale was attended by the Duke & Duchess of York on 12th September 1987?

SN What percentage of alcohol by volume will you find in a can of *Grolsch*?

SL What first gained swimmer Gertrude Ederle a place in the record books?

152

G Which city is the setting for *Kojak*?

E What are the first names of comedy duo French and Saunders?

H Which lawyer broke the law by refusing to be finger-printed in the Transvaal during 1907?

AL Who, in 1974, became the first Soviet citizen to be expelled from his country since Trotsky in 1929?

SN What do gypsies serve up under the name 'hotchi-witchi'?

SL Who scored 405 for Worcestershire against Somerset in 1988?

153

G What are the three colours of the German flag?

E What is Mike Baldwin served with if he asks for "the usual" in the *Rovers Return*?

H Which great battle took place from 1st July to 18th November 1916?

AL Which famous bear lives in Nutwood?

SN For her work with which vegetable did Barbara McClintock win a 1983 Nobel Prize?

SL How many World championship points is a Grand Prix win worth?

154

G Which is the largest of the Benelux countries?

E Which TV newsreader was once the editor of the *Daily Express*?

H How many arms does the South African Neo-Nazi party's swastika-like symbol have?

AL Which American writer described Wagner's music as being "better than it sounds"?

SN What type of bacteria caused hysteria when it was found in soft cheeses in 1989?

SL What horse did Steve Cauthen cut to success on in the 1985 Oaks, the 1000 Guineas and the St. Leger?.

155

G Which seaside resort offers picturesque views of Thatcher Rock?

E In what country was Anneka Rice born?

H Which monster legend first came into being in 1921 when large footprints were photographed in the snow?

AL What is the name of Hereford Cathedral's most famous map?

SN What were unsuccessfully launched as APTs in 1981?

SL Who won the 1986 Canadian Grand Prix?

156

G What is the official language of Papua New Guinea?

E Which popular BBC Radio presenter died of cancer in 1989?

H Which US university saw National Guardsmen open fire on its students in 1970?

AL What was Bob Hope's book *Confession of a Hooker* about?

SN How many of the nine major planets are named after gods?

SL Which cricketer was dropped for two months for admitting that he'd smoked dope when he was a student?

157

G What is the official language of Chile?

E What game takes place in a sewer in *Guys and Dolls*?

H Which Swedish Prime Minister was shot dead as he walked home through Stockholm?

AL As what is the most frequently played segment from Wagner's *Lohengrin* known?

SN Which month gives its name to hawthorn blossom?

SL Who are second to Russia in the all-time Winter Olympics medals table?

158

G Which continent has the highest mountain outside Asia?

E What is folk singer Peggy Seeger's pop singing daughter called?

H Which Scottish town was devastated after a mid-air explosion on a Boeing 747?

AL Who commissioned this famous embroidery, and what is its name?

SN Which Apollo mission took the first man to the moon?

SL Which trophy has been won by *Columbia*, *Constellation* and *Intrepid*?

159

G Which city was the capital of British India until 1912?

E Which is the surname of radio characters Phil and Jill, who called their children Shula, David, Elizabeth and Kenton?

H Why did the so called FREE Presbyterian Church of Scotland ban Lord Mackay from their services?

AL Which of his operas did Sullivan have to re-write in America because he'd left the music in England?

SN What aid to grooming was invented by Colonel Jacob Schick in 1928?

SL What year saw the first golf shot on the moon?

160

G Which river is nicknamed 'Old Muddy'?

E What were Paula Wilcox and Richard Beckinsale according to a TV programme title?

H Whose 80th birthday was celebrated by a 1980 service in St. Paul's Catherdal?

AL Who wrote *1985*?

SN Which two months are named after men who actually lived?

SL What nationality is ex-world motor racing champion Keke Rosberg?

161

G What is the second letter in the name Florence if you come from Italy?

E What is the real life relationship between *My Husband and I* stars William Moore and Mollie Sugden?

H What position was held by Javiar Perez de Cuellar in 1991?

AL In what century was the Domesday Book written?

SN What kind of fruit was named after Enoch Bartlett?

SL What annually televised sporting event always brings a commentary mention for Craven Steps?

162

G After which George was Georgia named?

E What naval rank did *Only Fools and Horses* character Uncle Albert attain?

H Which quartet issued the *Limehouse Declaration*?

AL Who is your idol if you are a 'Bardologist'?

SN For which theory of the creation is Georges Lemaitre famous?

SL Who said: "that business with Hitler didn't bother me, I didn't go there to shake hands with him anyway"?

163

G In which Egyptian town was the Rosetta Stone found?

E What was the name of Jill Chance's *Crossroads* brother?

H Who was sitting on the end of the Queen's bed when her maid said: "Bloody hell, Ma'am what's going on here"?

AL Who wrote the James Bond novel *Colonel Sun* under the pseudonym Robert Markham?

SN What do pangolins eat?

SL What trap is a greyhound running from if it's in black and white stripes in England and orange in Ireland?

164

G Which member of the Royal Family was born in the Hampshire village of Dummer?

E What was the number of the house where Ethel hosted her weekly *Sandwich Quiz*?

H Where did a court rule that women were breaking the law by camping on a common because the common they were camping on wasn't a common?

AL Which royal's portrait by Brian Organ was carved up by both the critics and a slasher?

SN What dangerous insulation material is known as the 'woolly rock'?

SL As what did Everton Weekes become Barbados' champion, after retiring as his country's cricket captain?

165

G Which island's natives are called Vectians?

E What repeated word forms the total lyrical content of the *Entertainment USA* signature tune?

H Which organisation said to Mrs Thatcher: "We only have to be lucky once. You have to be lucky always"?

AL What weapon did *The Ancient Mariner* use to shoot down the albatross?

SN What is the alternative name for Indian corn?

SL What is the first name of cricket captain Colin Cowdrey's test cricketing son?

166

G Which river's estuary boasts Foulness Island?

E Where did Dr Zachary Smith get *Lost* ?

H Which British politician was held at gunpoint after landing at the wrong airport in 1988?

AL What is the Bayeux Tapestry if it isn't a tapestry (and it isn't)?

SN What is measured with a Dines Tilting Syphon?

SL Who was the VIP tosser who started the 1985 Baseball World Series?

167

G Which is the largest city on Lake Michigan?

E Which quiz show became a programme in its own right, after first appearing as part of *Wednesday Night Out*?

H What colour shirts did Garibaldi's followers wear?

AL In what kind of building did Miss Marple solve her first murder?

SN What was the date and time when all of the digits on a ten digit watch were displayed in numerical order?

SL What was the venue for the 1990 World Snooker championships?

168

G What collective name is given to 25th March, 24th June, 29th September and 25th December?

E Who went from the Ponderosa to *Battlestar Galactica*?

H How did Mussolini travel to Rome during his 1922 March on Rome?

AL During what month did Robert Browning have a longing to be in England?

SN What is the largest real animal to have a year dedicated to it in the Chinese calendar?

SL What kind of sports field does John Lennon help to create in the desert, in the film *How I Won the War*?

169

G Which American tourist attraction can be viewed from boats called *Maid of the Mist*?

E Who lives at 25B Foxbury Court, Gloucester Road, London?

H What was the last capital to be liberated from the Germans at the end of World War II?

AL Which film star's statue stands in London's Leicester Square?

SN What metal was used in early flash photography because it burns with a brilliant light?

SL How many pieces of wooden equipment are required to play cricket?

170

G Which national park has a visitor's centre at Grassington?

E What did the letters *B.S.B.* originally mean to a telly addict?

H Which first name was shared by French kings known as the Bald, the Fat and the Simple?

AL Which artist's funeral was marked by the hanging of wreaths in the mouths of the Trafalgar Square lions in October 1873?

SN What feature gives this creature the name 'conchiferous'?

SL Due to what was the 1974 Monte Carlo Rally cancelled?

171

G Which mountain is directly above your head if you are playing this game in the world's longest motor tunnel?

E Who split in December 1983 and then reformed for *Live Aid*?

H Which British prime minister was one-sixteenth Iroquois Indian?

AL What were readers asked to discover for themselves in Kit Williams' follow-up to *Masquerade*?

SN What name was given to the winged dinosaur discovered in 1871 by O.C.Marsh?

SL Which year first saw FA Cup Final receipts top two million pounds?

172

G Which city is connected to London by the *Master Cutler* train service?

E Who played piano on Wham's final single?

H Who was Britain's last Hanoverian monarch?

AL How does Ophelia kill herself in *Hamlet*?

SN What are the two predominant colours of a wild budgerigar?

SL Which year saw the first all-seater FA Cup Final?

173

G On what can you sail in Oxford, that you can spend in Ireland?

E Which fictional children's character had a 10/6 price tag on his head?

H What part of his body did Captain Jenkins have pickled so that he could show it to Parliament in 1739?

AL To what novel was *Oliver's Story* the sequel?

SN Which mammal's species name is 'Delphinus delphis'?

SL Which shining example of a horse managed to grind its way to victory in all 5 Cheltenham Gold Cups from 1932 to 1936?

174

G Which was the first country to have a public monorail system?

E Which county can you visit for a pint in Daphne du Maurier's *Jamaica Inn*?

H What year saw the Dunkirk evacuation?

AL Whose *Rites of Passage* won him the 1980 Booker Prize?

SN Where would you see the mountains and seas that Johannes Hevelius mapped and named in the seventeenth century?

SL How many points do you lose for being landed with the letter X at the end of a game of *Scrabble*?

175

G Which is Europe's second busiest airport?

E Which film 'action man' was expelled from Eton?

H What costumes did the St. Valentines Day Massacre gunmen use as disguises?

AL What work finds Sebastian striking up a close relationship with Charles at Oxford?

SN What do scientists claim that most male sleepers do between 10 and 20 times each night?

SL Which yachting competition ends with the Fastnet race?

176

G Which London Underground line was opened 25 years after the Coronation?

E What could be heard between the tracks of Sigue Sigue Sputnik's debut album?

H Which future newsagent's name first hit the headlines as First Lord of the Admiralty in Disraeli's government?

AL Who was Jacob Marley's business partner?

SN With which drug did Sigmund Freud become fascinated, while experimenting with the treatment of neurasthenia?

SL What is four feet in front of the stumps in a game of cricket?

177

G How many locks are there in the Suez Canal?

E What can you do with the right combination of lovely things and fairy dust, according to Peter Pan?

H How many mutinies did Captain Bligh experience?

AL Which famous novelist was a World War I spy?

SN Who has the most chromosomes — Tarzan, Jane or Cheetah?

SL What is the total number of gold medals presented in the 1916, 1940 and 1944 Olympic Games?

178

G Which London station has the most platforms?

E What girl's name was a hit for Jonathan King and Laura Branigan?

H What is the second name of Princess Anne's son Peter?

AL What did Osirus use to conquer the world according to Greek mythology?

SN What did Jacques Edwin Brandenburger invent in 1908, in which he could have wrapped his sandwiches?

SL What is the cricketing term for a left-handed googly?

179

G Which London Underground line goes to Heathrow?

E Whose *Watching the Detectives* was the first hit single on the *Stiff* record label?

H What year saw the raising of the *Mary Rose*?

AL Who called her autobiography *Courting Triumph*?

SN What is the international radio code word for the letter E...E...E...E?

SL What is the cricketing term for an off-break bowled with a leg-break action?

180

G Which hills form most of the border between Avon and Somerset?

E Which American R'n'B rockers were known as C.C.R?

H What was privatised with slogan 'Tell Sid?'

AL How many women did the shark munch its way through in *Jaws*?

SN What kind of fronts are shown as points on lines on weather maps?

SL Which Olympic event involves throwing a 5lb 6.55oz object?

181

G Which American river flows through St.Paul and St.Louis?

E Which dancing duo's first film together was *Dancing Down to Rio*?

H Which British political party had the longest serving leader at the end of 1991?

AL Which Biblical character called his son Ham, despite his Jewish upbringing?

SN What is the science of the interaction between the air and solid bodies moving through it?

SL What piece of sporting equipment did Canadian astronaut Marc Garneau take into space?

182

G Which South American capital was famous as a source for pepper?

E Which 1962 movie opened with Peter O'Toole dying in a motorcycle accident and then saw him riding a camel?

H Of what was Edward Kennedy convicted after swimming away from the Chappaquiddick death scene?

AL In which language was *The Divine Comedy* written?

SN What does a man have removed if he has an orchidectomy?

SL How did Ferdi Adoboe run, to break the world 100 yards record in 12.8 seconds on 1983?

183

G What is the largest country in the world to boast a nine-letter name?

E What disaster featured in the 1930 film *Atlantic*?

H Which queen ordered Lady Jane Grey's execution?

AL Which Asian country is the setting for *Little Black Sambo*?

SN What are the three secondary colours?

SL Which South African-born Australian footballer was bought by Liverpool in 1981?

184

G Which country owns the Suez Canal?

E Which *Disney* movie included the song *The Bear Necessities*?

H Which year saw the wearing of seat belts become compulsory for British drivers?

AL In which country is *A Midsummer Night's Dream* dreamed?

SN What sort of beans are most usually used to produce bean sprouts?

SL At what sport did this man compete at international level?

185

G In which country would you be if you were at the farthest point in the world from the sea?

E Which major 1970 box-office success centered on the relationship between characters played by Ryan O'Neal and Ali MacGraw?

H This man was head of which organisation?

AL When are the only occasions that *Catch-22* characters are allowed to go in to see Major Major?

SN Is marble a sedimentary, igneous or metamorphic rock?

SL Which British racecourse gives its name to courses in Perth, Australia and Toronto, Canada?

186

G Which continent includes six countries crossed by the Equator?

E Which pop star received a special mention from the organisers of the 1986 Nobel Peace Prize?

H Who said: "I have signed legislation today that will outlaw Russia forever. We begin bombing in five minutes"?

AL What is the Ministry of Peace responsible for, in the novel *Nineteen Eighty-Four*?

SN What pops out of a cicada's ovipositor?

SL Which trophy was Ronald Reagan referring to when he said: "Don't bolt that cup down too tightly"?

187

G Which is the only US state due south of Alaska?

E Which newspaper launched a Ferry Aid single that managed to include large-chested Linda Lusardi in its list of 'pop stars'?

H What did America's tacky *National Enquirer* ask Dr. Christiaan Barnard to transplant, for a $250,000 fee in 1979?

AL Who, in 1948, became the first American-born poet to win the Nobel Prize for literature?

SN Which major planet comes closest to the Earth?

SL What meat is chopped into a traditional Quiche Lorraine?

188

G Which country boasts San Marcos University; the oldest active university in the Americas?

E What is 'heaven' according to Belinda Carlisle?

H Who was the first US president to have a brother in the Senate?

AL Under what name did 18th-century Frenchman Francois-Marie Arouet write?

SN How many years make a lustrum?

SL How many different squares are open to a knight making the very first move in a game of chess?

189

G Which city is the home of New Zealand's House of Representatives?

E Which muscle-bound actor played the robot in *The Terminator*?

H Which famous pilot was shot down over Vaux-sur-Seine, France on 21st April 1918?

AL Which poet's "Tiger'" was "burning bright"?

SN Which company was ordered to perform safety checks on 1,755 of its jets in 1989?

SL What two drinks combine to make a Spritzer?

190

G Which ocean's deepest point is the Puerto Rico Trench?

E Who is the main scriptwriter for the *Victoria Wood* series?

H Which Russian city endured Bloody Sunday on 5th January?

AL What is the singular of 'Genera'?

SN Where were Helen Sharman and Timothy Mace selected as the finalists, to become the first visiting British people?

SL What drink is a traditional cause of burnt lips, due to being served on fire with a floating coffee bean?

191

G Which politician is commemorated at a museum in Llanystumdwy, Wales?

E Which West Texas town was a hit for Marty Robins?

H What did William II, Richard I, Edward II, James I and William III all have a reputation for being?

AL Which alternative comedian called his first novel *Stark*?

SN What is the name for the ugly red fleshy appendage that hangs on the neck of a turkey?

SL Which famous cup is the world's oldest international sporting trophy?

192

G Which station is the London terminal of the Great Western Railway?

E What two-word phrase has provided the title for 12 American chart records?

H Which European country suffered a violent coup attempt in 1981?

AL Which Dickens work featured Mr and Mrs Micawber?

SN With what complaint do you sock-it to your partner, if you suffer podobromhidrosis?

SL Which local team does *EastEnders'* Arthur support?

193

G How many passenger terminals are there at Heathrow?

E Which comedian was Sherlock Holmes to Arthur Lowe's Watson?

H To what was Britain's school leaving age raised, in 1947?

AL Which famous writer's first names were Edward Morgan?

SN Which chemical element has the shortest name?

SL Which club's cap did W.G. Grace usually wear when playing cricket?

194

G What language is Romaic?

E Which of the six wives was played by Dorothy Tutin in TV's *The Six Wives of Henry VIII*?

H What made the news by getting themselves banned from the 1983 Chelsea Flower Show?

AL Which detective fell to his death over a waterfall and was revived eight years later?

SN Where do benthic marine animals live?

SL What game does Gregory Peck play with Mao Tse Tung in the film *The Most Dangerous Man In The World*?

195

G Which European capital is built on the banks of the Manzanares River?

E What series linked Nyree Dawn Porter, Tony Anholt and Robert Vaughan?

H Which judge presided over the trials following the Monmouth Rebellion?

AL Whose novel *The Birds* was filmed by Hitchcock?

SN What kind of creatures are African nightcrawlers?

SL How many Jacks in a pack of playing cards have two eyes?

196

G Which US state boasts *EPCOT* Centre?

E What did *Fawlty Towers'* waiter Manuel call his pet rat?

H Who wrote: "I am down on whores and I shan't stop ripping them"?

AL For what delicate art form is the Devon town of Honiton famous?

SN Which scientist used to appear on the back of pound notes?

SL Which world heavyweight Boxing Champion's middle name was Marcellus?

G This city spans two continents. What is it and which two continents does it encompass?

E Who starred in *Falcon Crest* after seeing her former husband become president of the USA?

H To which newspaper did Sarah Tisdall leak?

AL Which work by Milton was delayed in publishing by the Great Plague and then by the Fire of London?

SN What creature gives us genuine sepia?

SL Who had the bear-faced-cheek to scream out during a world title fight: "Ma! He's killing me!"?

G Which geographical location was the very first word spoken from the moon?

E What did Mary Beth and Harvey Lacey call their first son?

H Which country had a Foreign Minister called Lee Bum Suk?

AL What number was the 'Protocol' that was a best seller for Frederick Forsyth?

SN What form of transport did the Montgolfier brothers invent?

SL How much did Jack Solomons bequeath to the British Boxing Board of Control when he died?

G Which US tourist attraction is known as the 'Shrine of Democracy'?

E Which TV character drives a car with the registration number J 1610?

H What nickname did Margaret Thatcher pick up after constantly saying: "There Is No Alternative"?

AL Which novel preceded *Paradise Regained*?

SN How many zeros follow the number 1 to form a googol?

SL For what sport did Sports Minister Colin Moynihan win an Olympic silver medal?

G Which sands off the Kent coast are known as 'The Widow Maker'?

E What industry featured in the TV mini-series *Bare Essence*?

H Who married both Margaret Kempson and Margaret Roberts?

AL Who is married to her co-presenter John Stapleton?

SN Who was left orbiting the moon while Armstrong was getting all of the glory with his 'one small step for man'?

SL Who was the first captain to oppose Emlyn Hughes' team on *A Question of Sport*?

201

G As what is the 9th century kingdom of Alba now known?

E Which '70s pop group included Rick Wakeman and the Hudson Ford duo in its union?

H Who celebrated his 40th birthday in 1987 with 1500 guests in a converted tram shed near Aston Villa football ground?

AL Which Moody Blues album takes its title from the famous mnemonic, spelling out the lines of the treble stave?

SN What was W.H.Carrier's real cool invention?

SL Which brewery sponsored the 1987 Melbourne Cup?

202

G What is the closest county to the Isle of Wight?

E What competitive failure did Norway achieve in 1963, 1978 and 1981 that was equalled by Finland in 1963, 1965 and 1982?

H What title was given to Harold Macmillan on his 90th birthday?

AL Where does *Carousel* begin?

SN Which season begins with the vernal equinox?

SL Which sport was won by Argentina when it was finally chucked out of the Olympics in 1936?

203

G Which country's national flower is the wattle?

E Which chart-topper spent his 1985 birthday on a hijacked *TWA* aircraft?

H Which ship spent 437 years on the seabed off Southsea?

AL Which patriotic pop song creeps in at the end of the *New World Symphony*?

SN What was created by the Manhattan Project?

SL How many gymnastic Olympic gold medals had Britain won up to and including the 1988 games?

204

G Which river forms most of the boundary between Mexico and the USA?

E Which Walt Disney character's body is modelled on this famous actress?

H Who was the only female member of Edward Heath's cabinet when he first became Prime Minister?

AL Who said of American football: "It has become so complicated that students will find it a recreation to go to classes"?

SN Which of the major planets isn't named after a god?

SL Who called the County Cricket Board selectors "Gin-slinging dodderers"?

205

G What do 100 Egyptian piastres make?

E What is Rumpole's first name?

H Who resigned as Britain's Secretary of State for War in 1963?

AL Which French writer said: "Everything I know about morals I learnt on the football field"?

SN From where exactly would you remove the offending object if you had a glob of something stuck in your philtrum?

SL How many times did Bjorn Borg win the Wimbledon men's singles?

206

G Which English county boasts the longest stretch of coastline?

E Who was the first *Coronation Street* regular to move to the new Docklands development?

H Which British royal took tea with Adolf Hitler?

AL Of what form of artistic expression is Caedmon the first named British exponent?

SN What did Russell Doig do on the River Thames in 1983 that hadn't been done there for 150 years?

SL What is your sport if you lift the Heisman Trophy?

207

G As what is the Gulf of Gascony now known?

E What was the name of the Prime Minister in *Yes Prime Minister*?

H Where did suffragette Emily Davison die?

AL Who appeared on *Jackanory* reading his own book *The Old Man of Lochnagar*?

SN What do girasol plants turn towards?

SL Which British race track would you visit to see 'Clearways'?

208

G Which city saw work start on its own version of Disneyworld in 1989?

E Which colourful band of the '60s and '70s recorded *Live at Pompeii*?

H Which city was devastated first by an earthquake and then by a fire in April 1906?

AL Who did John Betjeman succeed as Poet Laureate?

SN What is the most distant planet from the Sun?

SL Which trophy did John Jeffrey damage to earn a five month suspension from rugby?

209

G In which state was the Charleston born?

E Which band took their name from Mr. Spock's Vulcan friend on *Star Trek*?

H What precious stone represents the wedding anniversary that the Queen celebrated in 1987?

AL Which London building with strong Dickensian connections was put up for sale in 1988?

SN What was Samuel Benedict trying to cure when he ordered his first Eggs Benedict?

SL Which London stadium was built for the 1908 Anglo-French Exhibition and later used for the 1908 Olympics?

210

G Which major Danish tourist attraction is built out of miniature bricks?

E Which actress won an Oscar for her role in the 1938 film *Jezebel*?

H What event pulled the world's biggest TV audience on 13th July 1985?

AL In what material is Rene Lalique best remembered for his work?

SN In which country did the *R101* airship make its maiden flight?

SL Which 'British' athlete was disqualified in the 1984 Olympic women's 3000 metres?

211

G Which county includes most of the Cotswold range?

E Which Scottish rocker styled himself 'Sensational' and once had a role in *Hair*?

H Why did Monica Coghlan make headlines in 1986?

AL Which city sees Hyman Roth's birthday celebrations in *The Godfather, Part II*?

SN What insecticide was discovered in 1939 by Paul Muller?

SL How many players should be in the pool at any one time during an Olympic water polo match?

212

G In what is Midway Island midway?

E Who went round nicking knickers off washing lines and was a hit for Pink Floyd?

H Who made headlines in 1987 when two of her first cousins, previously listed as dead, were found living in a mental home?

AL What is the name of Captain Kremmen's large-breasted buddy?

SN What did Victorian women try to enlarge by massaging with crushed strawberries?

SL Who was the grandfather of Gina Hemphill who carried the Olympic torch into the 1984 Los Angeles' Olympic stadium?

213

G Which Australian anti-hero gave rise to the tourist industry in the town of Glenrowan?

E What was the name of the Beatles' own film label which released *Magical Mystery Tour*?

H Who was the only one of Henry VIII's wives to survive him?

AL Which 19th century Polish pianist and composer has been called 'The poet of the piano'?

SN In what do monotheists believe?

SL Who sang *All Night Long* at the 1984 Los Angeles Olympics closing ceremony?

214

G Which European city tags its airport bags CPH?

E What gave the pilot food poisoning in *Airplane*?

H Who was listed as Britain's wealthiest musician in a 1991 *Sunday Times* survey?

AL Which American poet was such a recluse that she often spoke to her guests from an adjoining room?

SN Which bird is considered to be sacred in Sweden due to its legendary presence at the Crucifixion?

SL What do the letters R.S.C. stand for after the result of an Olympic boxing match?

215

G Which country would you visit to drink *Budweiser* in Budweis?

E Who said: "I race cars, I play tennis, I fondle women, but I have weekends off"?

H Where were the Macdonalds massacred?

AL Why is the date 22nd September of significance to Frodo and Bilbo in *Lord of the Rings*?

SN What is the Spanish word for sun-dried clay brick?

SL Which ground is the headquarters of Welsh rugby?

216

G Where would you go to see the site of the bunker where Hitler had his final bunk up?

E What did James Cagney say he was "on top of" in the 1948 movie *White Heat*?

H How many times had the Duchess of Windsor married before she married Edward VIII?

AL How many ducats did this Shakespearean character loan to Antonio?

SN How many dimensions does the shadow of a three-dimensional object have?

SL Which Grand Slam tennis tournament is played south of the Equator?

217

G Which country do you look out to if you are viewing across the Formosa Strait from Taiwan?

E Which 1969 film featured an otter called Mitch?

H Which country's royal house is Bourbon-Parma?

AL What four words precede "In the forests of the night"?

SN What is five percent of 25?

SL What is mixed with *Tia Maria* to produce a *Tia Moo Moo*?

218

G Which country would you be in if you suffered from Bali Belly?

E What product's 1987 TV ads were backed by Ben E King's *Stand By Me* and Percy Sledge's *When A Man Loves A Woman*?

H Which president's profile appears on a US 1-cent coin?

AL What did Adrian Mole suffer from in the title of the second book about his teenage life?

SN What is the normal method of movement for a macropod?

SL What does a collector of coins call the side with the monarch's portrait on?

219

G Which country claims the world's largest fresh water supply?

E What word preceded *Colours* for Cyndi Lauper in the same chart as it preceded *Blue* for Madonna?

H What shape was the special 1969 Gibraltar halfpenny stamp?

AL Which pop singer was the subject of the 19th March 1984 *Time* magazine cover painted by Andy Warhol?

SN What masticatory substance did Thomas Adams invent while working on a substitute for rubber?

SL On how many pieces of apparatus are male Olympic gymnasts expected to perform after the completion of the floor exercises?

220

G Which country's name is used by *Private Eye* to mean sexual relations?

E Which village boasts the nearest pub to Emmerdale Farm?

H Who was Secretary-General of the United Nations during the Six Day War?

AL What is the name of the mansion in *Brideshead Revisited*?

SN Which element makes up 89 percent of water's weight?

SL Which English fast bowler took the most wickets in the 'Bodyline' series?

221

G Which African country has a province called Buganda?

E Which popular cartoon strip was turned into a musical by Alan Price?

H Which goddess was the chief protectress of ancient Athens?

AL In which castle is Rudolf held prisoner, in an 1894 Anthony Hope story?

SN What gas is rapidly released from the blood and tissues to give a diver the bends when he comes to the surface too quickly?

SL Which sport provided Cuba's Teofilo Stevenson with three consecutive Olympic golds?

222

G Would you be allowed to use a French stamp to post a French letter in a French envelope from Monaco?

E Which TV series featured Miranda Richardson as Elizabeth I?

H Which Russian leader was quoted as saying: "Life is short, live it up"?

AL Which literary classic follows the search for a seven-hundred-thousand pound treasure of gold?

SN Which planet was found to have three previously undiscovered moons by *Voyager II*?

SL Who won the most Wimbledon men's singles titles in the 1970s?

223

G Which British port claims to be the busiest in the world?

E Who was Vicky's dad on *EastEnders*?

H On what day of the week are budgets traditionally read?

AL Which best-selling book was the combined effort of a committee of 47 people?

SN What name is given to the flowers of willow and poplar trees?

SL How many horses have won the famous double of the Derby and the Grand National?

224

G Which famous racing town is close to Tintern Abbey?

E Which female comedy character's surname was Morgenstern?

H Which day of the week saw the official start of World War II?

AL How old was Lolita when Professor Humbert first fell for her?

SN How many phalanges, or finger bones, are there in a normal human hand?

SL What was Elvis Presley's sport in *Kid Galahad*?

225

G What is the capital of Southern Australia?

E What two letters followed the name of Trapper John in *M*A*S*H*?

H What were the first two British coins to be minted with decimal values?

AL What was Cinderella's first name?

SN What kind of poisoning is known as 'plumbism'?

SL What sport featured in *Damn Yankees*?

226

G Which is the only European city-state to claim a zero birthrate?

E Which town is the home of firemen Hugh, Pugh, Barney, McGrew, Cuthbert, Dibble and Grub?

H What single name is used by Ian Kilminster of Motorhead?

AL Into what kind of animal was Pinocchio temporarily turned?

SN What is the name of this planet?

SL Which boxer has a surname that can be repeated to become the name of a pop group?

227

G Which is the only US state that ends with the letter G?

E Which show introduced Lou Grant?

H Who was the daughter of a prime minister, the mother of a prime minister and was also a prime minister herself?

AL What begins: "If music be the food of love"?

SN Which was the first spacecraft to go up and down and up and down again?

SL What might you have in a hotel that has the same name as a darts score of 26?

228

G Which European country's capital is Vilnius?

E Which comedy series featured the Trotter family?

H What name had a man adopted by deed poll that resulted in his being banned from standing in the 1983 election for Finchley?

AL What was Hiawatha's wife called?

SN Which was the third country to launch a rocket into space successfully ?

SL Which motor racing circuit is nicknamed the 'Brickyard'?

229

G Which English county precedes its name with 'Royal'?

E What once accidentally popped out when Kenneth Kendall was reading the news?

H Which country's embassy objected, in 1982, to the use of the word 'Mongol' when describing Down's Syndrome?

AL What was Miss Marples first name?

SN What did William Morris repair before he started to build cars?

SL Which steeplechase has the longest run of sponsorship of any British horserace?

230

G What is mainland Europe's most heavily populated city?

E What are repaired in the shop in which *Bullman* is based?

H Which former First Lady was 'frankly' not amused by Kitty Kelley's unauthorised biography?

AL Which American tourist attraction was carved by Gutzon Borglum?

SN What vitamin deficiency was chiefly responsible for scurvy?

SL What is the final event of a triathlon?

231

G Which American state has orange blossom as its official flower?

E Who was the goodie-goodie presenter of *The Fame Game*?

H What was unusual about the Roman Consul Incitatus?

AL Which mutiny was directed against Captain Queeg?

SN What is the only breed of female deer with antlers?

SL What was the first sport to be covered by a British radio broadcast?

232

G What popular abbreviation is used for the Caribbean islands of Aruba, Bonaire and Curacao?

E Who temporarily left his desert island to ask people about their *Favourite Things* on television?

H What is the first name of Ferdinand Marcos' widow?

AL On whose novel was the TV mini-series *Lace* based?

SN What is the second largest planet?

SL Which famous showjumper is the brother of show jumping Liz Edgar?

233

G Over which Indian building are aircraft banned from flying?

E What kind of animal was Ermintrude?

H Which Labour MP lost his front bench trade and industry post for taking a part-time job on Sky television?

AL What kind of instrument is an English horn?

SN What was the name of the first manned module to land on the moon?

SL What were Foinavon's odds when it won the 1967 Grand National?

234

G What is the main link between theatrical blood and the road that runs past the Albert Hall?

E Who had a 1990 hit with *Infinity* and sounded like he should have been on an Indian take-away menu?

H Who succeeded Keir Hardie as Chairman of the Labour Party?

AL Whose *Weeping Woman* fetched over three million pounds in 1987?

SN What did Joseph Gayetty develop in the 19th century in an attempt to prevent haemorrhoids?

SL Which pop legend always won at *Scrabble* because he only allowed his opponents 5 tiles?

235

G Which country calls itself Helvetia on its stamps?

E Which American singer was nicknamed 'Swoonlight'?

H What killed 400 people in New York on 2nd July 1901?

AL Which famous partner of Nijinsky died in 1931, just a few days before her 50th birthday?

SN What was the popular name for the vertical take off machine officially called the Rolls-Royce Thrust Measuring Rig?

SL Which British sportsman attracted the headline 'The Eagle Has Landed' in 1988?

236

G What do Falkland Islanders call '365' because they eat it every day of the year?

E Who made his film debut in the 1914 movie *Making A Living*?

H In which decade of the 20th Century did *Lego* building blocks first come on to the market?

AL What nationality was Henrik Ibsen?

SN Who was the first person to fly in an aircraft?

SL What nickname did Voce and Larwood's aggressive bowling give to the 1933 England tour of Australia?

(237)

G Which motorway from the West Country meets the M4 just outside Bristol?

E What was Steven Spielberg's 1980 reworking of *Close Encounters* called?

H What is Napoleon's final word said to have been?

AL Whose *The Longest Journey* led to a *Room With A View* and *A Passage to India*?

SN Who opened her first London birth control clinic in 1921?

SL What, in 1984, did most of the Eastern Bloc describe as "a commercialised US propaganda exercise"?

(238)

G Which city would you visit to see the *Colman's* Mustard Shop?

E What name was a major 50s hit for Elias and his Zig Zag Jive Flutes?

H Who did Lord Halifax think was a butler and give his hat to when they first met in 1937?

AL Where, if anywhere, is the apostrophe in *Reader's Digest*?

SN What breaks when its height is three quarters of its depth?

SL Which sport was devised by Major Killander?

(239)

G What is the difference between the American spelling and the British spelling of the word centre?

E What was Carla Thomas's four hyphenated letter hit title?

H Whose third wife was Calpurnia?

AL Which city is the setting for Puccini's *La Boheme*?

SN What was the first year in the 20th century that Halley's Comet was visible, with the naked eye, from earth?

SL How many metres long is an official Olympic running track?

(240)

G Who based one of his best-known TV characters on the owner of a hotel in this Devon holiday resort?

E Who changed his middle name from Winston to Ono on 22nd April 1969?

H What female name was given to the 1914 Defence Of the Realm Act?

AL Which tenor took a stab at becoming a movie star in *Yes, Giorgio*?

SN How many days of the week occur 53 times in a leap year?

SL Who made headlines in 1990 by falling off a polo pony?

241

G Which river flows under Florence's *Ponte Vecchio*?

E Which film features a computer called *HAL* who gets very upset when Dave tries to turn him off?

H Who did Bob Ford kill for a $10,000 reward in 1882?

AL Who was the first person to see the risen Jesus?

SN Which element, also called wolfram, can be used as the filament in electric light bulbs?

SL How many balls get racked at the start of a game of pool?

242

G How many republics made up the former Soviet Union?

E Which of the *Star Trek* movies was subtitled *The Search For Spock*?

H What was US presidential candidate Walter Mondale's nickname?

AL Which girl and her pet became the subject of an eight-line poem by Sarah Hale?

SN What kind of animals can be horseshoe, broad-nosed and long-eared?

SL What was this boxer's honey of a catchphrase?

243

G Which country's possessions in Africa are Ceuta and Melilla?

E Who played Sam Spade in the 1941 version of *The Maltese Falcon*?

H Which was the first major city to be bombed by aeroplanes in August 1914?

AL Which American mystery writer gave us the line: "The glory that was Greece, and the grandeur that was Rome"?

SN What is the oldest man-made metal?

SL What event did 37-year-old Carlos Lopez win to become the oldest gold medallist in the 1984 Los Angeles Olympics?

244

G Which is the only republic with the Union Jack on its flag?

E Which was the first UK TV channel to show a triangle in the screen corner to warn of sexy films?

H Which mass murderer tried to stab his trial judge with a sharpened pencil?

AL Which character in *A Christmas Carol* is "as good as gold"?

SN What disease afflicted 82 percent of those who worked on the Panama Canal in 1906?

SL Which number was voted the best when experts judged 100 numbered vats of Scotch whisky in 1863?

245

G What is the name for the parallel of north latitude at 66 degrees, 33 minutes?

E Which album's birthday was celebrated by a 1987 TV programme called *It Was Twenty Years Ago Today*?

H What title was shared by Jiang Qing, Wang Hong-wen, Zhang Cun-qiao and Yao Wen-yuan, and David, Shirley, Roy and Bill?

AL With whom was Adrian Mole profoundly in love?

SN Which flower is associated with Easter Sunday?

SL What is the value of Pontoon in the card game of that name?

246

G Which distillery in Lynchburg, Tennessee, has been declared a US national historic place?

E Which recording studio held the official *Sgt Pepper* 20th anniversary party?

H Which is the only country in the world to have removed all nuclear weapons from its arsenal?

AL What did the Walrus and the Carpenter weep "like anything to see such quantities of"?

SN Which is smallest: a microsecond, a nanosecond or a picosecond?

SL What does a trotter do if it breaks?

247

G How many stars twinkled on the Soviet Union's flag?

E What is this lovely lady's name, and who is the actor playing her?

H In what country was U.N. Secretary-General Javier Perez de Cuellar born?

AL Which popular eastern Mediterranean holiday island sees the death of Othello?

SN What was the exact date in 1968 when Apollo 8 astronauts became the first humans to see the far side of the moon?

SL What score do you have to reach to win a singles match in lawn bowls?

248

G What animal holds the sword on the flag of Sri Lanka?

E Who does *Halliwell's Film Goer's Guide* list as "American muscle man who took to acting"?

H Which organisation accepted the responsibility for killing *Guinness Book of Records'* editor Ross McWhirter?

AL Which member of the *Peanuts* gang gets called "Sweet Baboo" by Sally?

SN Which letter and numbers signify a US Tomcat jet?

SL How many Community Chest cards are there in *Monopoly*?

(249)

G What is the capital of South Africa's Cape Province?

E What TV duo is played by Sharon Gless and Tyne Daly?

H Which country was Benito Mussolini trying to reach when he was killed by Italian partisans?

AL Which saga's first book is called *A Man of Property*?

SN Which car company bought out *Jaguar* in 1989?

SL What is your sport if two waza-aris equal ippon, but no number of yukos or kokas can ever equal waza-aris?

(250)

G Which London Underground line is coloured green on a map?

E What was the relationship between the characters played by Marlon Brando and Rod Steiger in *On The Waterfront*?

H In which year did these protestors march upon London?

AL How did Captain Hook lose his hand?

SN What did pessimistic Hyman L. Lipman add to pencils in 1858?

SL Who, in 1975, became the first English football club banned from international competition due to its hooligan supporters?

(251)

G What do Italians wait for at a stazione ferroviaria?

E What was Frank Spencer's daughter called?

H How many different prime ministers did Britain have in the 1960s?

AL What artistic technique involves painting directly onto wet plaster?

SN Which element was named by Martin Heinrich Klaproth in 1789 after a newly discovered planet?

SL What word links a cricket over with no runs and a horse that hasn't won a race?

(252)

G What national symbol is common to China and Wales?

E Which comedy series starred Diana Coupland as Sid James's wife?

H Who was America's first Republican president?

AL What exactly was *Sophie's Choice*?

SN How many carats is gold that has been assessed at 916 parts per thousand?

SL Which boxer sang with the Knockouts pop group?

253

G Which Serbian city's name means 'White City'?

E Which *Star Trek* role is filled by George Takei?

H Who succeeded Charles I as King of England?

AL Which successful 1982 film was based on Philip K.Dick's novel *Do Androids Dream of Electric Sheep*?

SN What did Marvin Chester Stone invent in 1886 when he hand-rolled a length of paraffin-coated Manila paper?

SL What bingo number is known as 'Sunset Strip'?

254

G Which major river flows through Baghdad?

E What stops the bus in *Bus Stop*?

H Which Labour MP made history by being the first to speak on televised House of Commons TV in 1989?

AL Which major art museum is built on the site of a 12th century fortress constructed by Philip-Augustus?

SN What name is given to the major belts of radiation around the Earth?

SL Which club received the money when Trevor Francis became Britain's first million pound footballer?

255

G What is the name of the 7100 island group on the eastern boundary of the South China Sea between Taiwan and eastern Indonesia?

E Who paid $150 to dance with Mrs. Charles Hamilton in *Gone With the Wind*?

H Which motor company did the Government sell after giving an alleged £38 million to British Aerospace, the buyers?

AL Which Lancashire-born rent collector and clerk took up painting full time when he retired in 1952?

SN What measurement unit is used to describe the brightness of a star?

SL Which Brazilian was world motor racing champion in 1972 and 1974?

256

G Which is Tibet's 'Forbidden City'?

E What was Minnie Caldwell's pussy on *Coronation Street* called?

H Which US Vice-President joined the Indiana National Guard when he could have been in Vietnam?

AL What did Vincenzo Perugia smuggle out of the Louvre?

SN What company was named in memory of an idyllic summer that Steve Jobs spent fruit-picking in Oregon?

SL In what sport would you be taking part, if you were on the piste but were not skiing?

257

G Where is the biggest submarine base in the Mediterranean?

E Who did Dan Aykroyd call "a good man, but a bad boy"?

H Which European gate was symbolically opened to celebrate Christmas 1989?

AL Which artist's painting *The Absinthe Drinker* was rejected when he submitted it to the Paris Salon?

SN Of what is the Montessori System a method?

SL Which athlete was known as the 'Pied Piper of Gateshead'?

258

G Which US state produces the most sugar cane?

E Which *Star Wars* character gave his name to the club seen early in the movie *Indiana Jones and the Temple of Doom*?

H What became one nation again on 3rd October, 1990?

AL Which word now means a great work of art but originally meant a work which demonstrated that a craftsman had completed his training?

SN What was the official name of the Doodlebug flying bomb?

SL What did 1966 World Cup footballer Ray Wilson do for a living when his soccer career finally died?

259

G Which country's third-largest city is Nagoya?

E What was the name of 'Pete's Dragon'?

H What date in 1989 saw a firing squad give Nicolae Ceausescu and his wife a present of a hail of bullets?

AL What nationality was the artist Joan Miro?

SN Where do you measure from, and to, if you want to know the screen size of a television set?

SL Which film saw Pele and Bobby Moore playing with Sylvester Stallone?

260

G Which is the largest Arabic-speaking country in Asia?

E Who was leader of the American Army-Air Force Band in Europe during World War II?

H Which British coin was introduced by Henry VIII who called it a 'Testoon'?

AL Which supermarket chain shares its name with the wing of the National Gallery that was begun in 1988?

SN What is the alternative name for oil of vitriol?

SL Which managerial roll did Ernest Borgnine fill in the Muhammad Ali movie *The Greatest*?

261

G What is the largest town in Britain that doesn't enjoy city status?

E What do they call the steward at the Winchester club in *Minder*?

H Which northern truck driver claimed to have seen visions in a graveyard?

AL Which film man's autobiography was called *Roman*?

SN What did the Russians claim to have working again in October 1986?

SL How many times do the cars go round the two and a half mile circuit to complete the Indianapolis 500?

262

G Which former concentration camp was converted into a home for Carmelite nuns?

E Whose 1990 album was called *Music From Graffiti Bridge*?

H Which political party was abolished in Romania on 1st January, 1990?

AL What is the better known name of Beethoven's *Piano Sonata in C sharp major*?

SN What do pisciculturists do?

SL Which Olympic event can include a kip, a walkabout and a fishtail?

263

G How many Northern Irish cities are there?

E Where does Del Boy have an office, in addition to New York and Paris, according to the sign on the side of his van?

H What did philosopher Erasmus try to hide by wearing a padded cap?

AL What is Harold trying to do with an arrow in the Bayeux Tapestry?

SN What is dropping off if you are starting to desquamate?

SL Which golfer was voted sportsman of the decade 1960-1970 by American sports writers?

264

G Which African desert is famous as the home of bushmen?

E Who has sold far more records than anyone else on the *Paisley Park* record label?

H Who did Winston Churchill call a "bloodthirsty guttersnipe"?

AL Which Verdi opera sees two lovers burned alive?

SN What natural exotic food is called 'Black diamond'?

SL Which uses the smallest balls, British snooker, American snooker or pool?

265

G Which South American country was named after one of the continent's best-known patriots?

E Who was *Praying For Time* in the 1990 pop charts?

H Which country didn't receive its petrochemical pipes in 1990 because they were thought to be the barrel of a gun?

AL Which of Bizet's operatic heroines was stabbed to death by Don Jose?

SN What identifies an isosceles triangle?

SL Which came first, five pin bowling, nine pin bowling or ten pin bowling?

266

G Which river flows through Washington D.C.?

E What two letters preceded Hammer in the name of the *U Can't Touch This* hit?

H Who became the first royal to sue a newspaper when he won libel damages against *Today*?

AL Which wild-west character became the title of an Aaron Copeland opera?

SN Which element boils at the lowest temperature?

SL What is the British equivalent of the European winter game called Eisschiessen?

267

G What is the Hebrew name for the Jewish Day of Atonement?

E Which 1990s rock band featured a fat Elvis Presley lookalike singing Led Zeppelin songs to a reggae beat?

H How many passenger seats were there in a Spitfire?

AL Which opera singer made a name for herself by performing in a silly hat at Prince Charles' wedding?

SN What is the common alternative name for the black leopard?

SL Which Spaniard was the only European to win the Wimbledon men's singles during the 1960s?

268

G What was the Soviet Union's official tourist agency called?

E Which Herman's Hermits 1965 hit was revived in 1990 by Cliff Richard?

H For how many days did Lady Jane Grey rule?

AL Who was the Irish author of the play on which Richard Strauss based his opera *Salome*?

SN What is the British name for the Great Maple?

SL Which year in the '80s saw the first English League football match played on an artificial pitch?

269

G Which Thames Bridge would be the first to get wet if the new flood barrier failed to work?

E Which Dennis Potter TV series featured a sleuth with a very bad skin complaint?

H Which continent did Harold Macmillan say that 'winds of change' were blowing through?

AL Who did Welsh students claim was a "white able-bodied heterosexist male" and then asked for his name to be changed to 'Patel'?

SN What is the name of the world's largest meteor crater?

SL Which boxer had a tropical fish named after him?

270

G Which continent has the lowest highest mountain?

E Who played Batman in the 1989 film version?

H What military retreat was called "a miracle of deliverance" by Winston Churchill?

AL Which city would you visit to see the Burrell Collection?

SN What effect causes a vehicle's sound to change as it passes you?

SL Who was the owner of Devil's Elbow when it failed a dope test after winning a race at Worcester?

271

G Which island is known as Ellan Vannin to its natives?

E Which was the first TV soap to bore us with Sunday repeats?

H Who, in 1913, called Britain "The best country in the world for a rich man to live in"?

AL Which composer's *Four Seasons* was a 1990 top 5 album smash for Nigel Kennedy?

SN What is crossed with a cowslip to produce a polyanthus?

SL Which rugby league club plays at Thrum Hall?

272

G Which is the main mountain range affected by the Chinook warm dry wind system?

E What did Madonna want to feel on her behind in the song *Hanky Panky*?

H Which is Britain's largest trade union?

AL What is the name of this cat, and which part of him is the last to disappear?

SN What is there to every action, according to Newton's third Law of Motion?

SL Which year in the '50s saw the first floodlit Football League match?

273

G What are the first three numbers of an Inner-London dialling code if you ring from outside London?

E Which Mamas and Papas hit was rehashed by River City People in the 1990s?

H Which Nobel Peace Prize winner was internally exiled by the Soviet government in Gorky in 1980?

AL Which flighty Puccini title character's actual name is Cio Cio San?

SN What would a somatologist want to study if he invited you to his place of work?

SL Which London football ground was partly declared a Grade Two listed building in 1987?

274

G Which European country was declared a Republic in 1931?

E Who was accused of being drunk after her disastrous 1990 London Palladium comeback concert?

H Which London underground station was the scene of a tragic fire in 1987?

AL What did Prince Edward carry to his first day of work at The Really Useful Theatre Company that is normally found in a kitchen?

SN What year saw *Concorde's* 21st birthday celebrations?

SL Who beat Jess Willard to take the world heavyweight boxing title in 1919?

275

G Which city boasts Mahatma Gandhi Park?

E Who was the first member of the *EastEnders* cast to have a chart hit after plugging the song on the show?

H Which US president was nicknamed 'Dutch' in his younger days?

AL Which legendary king of Thebes inadvertently killed his own father, Laius, on the way home from Delphi?

SN Which planet boasts the most natural satellites?

SL What game includes twelve hotels and thirty-two houses?

276

G Which Latin American city's natives refer to themselves as 'Cariocas'?

E Which TV character was prisoner number 146739 in Wormwood Scrubs?

H Who was called "Sir Nobody" by the press when he challenged Margaret Thatcher for the Tory leadership?

AL What type of floor covering was used as a printing block by both Picasso and Matisse?

SN Which planet was named by 13-year-old Venetia Burney from Oxford?

SL How old was Prince Philip when he retired from playing polo?

277

G Which is the most northerly national capital in mainland Europe?

E Which is the only winner of the Best Picture Oscar with a four-letter name?

H What did the Post Office revive in 1989?

AL With what do most modern painters dilute their linseed oil, when using it as an oil painting medium?

SN Which planet's year is shorter than its day?

SL What sport did Prince Philip take up when he retired from playing polo?

278

G Which Ocean includes the Coral Sea?

E Which US state had Ratso finally reached when he died on the bus in *Midnight Cowboy*?

H What is Egypt's main port?

AL Which book is subtitled *A Lioness of Two Worlds*?

SN What is the largest North American rodent?

SL What race for the Little America's Cup?

279

G What is said to have been the site of the northernmost Pillar of Hercules?

E Which of the *Girls On Top* had Neil Kinnock on one of her pop videos?

H Who was the first British monarch to circumnavigate the globe?

AL Which well-known writer's first names were Thomas Stearns?

SN What does a tea-drinker's extensor digiti minimi manus extend?

SL What two factors prevent Frank Bruno from entering the famous 'Golden Gloves' boxing tournament?

280

G Which city calls itself 'Soulsville USA'?

E Who was *McMillan* if Susan St. James was the wife?

H What did David Blunkett take to a State Opening of Parliament that no-one had ever taken before?

AL Which month of the year is Renoir's middle name?

SN Which popular bird was named after what was wrongly thought to be its country of origin?

SL Which film ended with James Fox winning a race?

281

G Which is the most southerly national capital in mainland Europe?

E Which is the only city in the world where Wayne Newton could possibly get gigs for 30 weeks per year?

H Of which war did Bush and Gorbachev declare the end during their warm 1989 shipboard meeting off Malta?

AL Which north of England artist said: "Had I not been lonely, I should not have seen what I did"?

SN Who was the second man to walk on the moon?

SL Who was the first man to beat Muhammad Ali in a professional fight?

282

G In what country does the Rhine rise?

E Which comedy series features the Lumsden family?

H Who told a court in 1983: "People are motivated by greed and there are no moral values at all"?

AL How many of Jerome K. Jerome's *Three Men In A Boat* are actually named in the plot?

SN With what gas was the Hindenburg explosively filled?

SL Which US president tried to tell the Washington Redskins how to play football?

283

G Whose statue stands in front of the British embassy in Washington D.C.?

E Whose 1987 tour was called *Graceland*?

H Who was the father of David Kennedy, found dead in a Florida hotel room in 1984?

AL Which novel of ancient Rome, first published in 1889, is subtitled *A tale of the Christ*?

SN Which natural process gets its name from the Greek words meaning 'light' and 'together'?

SL Which English cricket captain was known as Lord Ted?

284

G What do the English call what the French call 'Îles Normandes'?

E Which TV soap's *Almost There* theme tune was a hit for Marty Webb?

H What two words appear on a Victoria Cross?

AL Which plague-ridden city was the setting for Boccaccio's *Decameron*?

SN How many satellites do Mercury and Venus boast between them?

SL Who is this extremely famous number 41, and what was he the first to achieve?

285

G Which country is home to the majority of Khmers?

E What role did Buddy Ebsen have to drop in 1939 because the metallic paint made him ill?

H Which was the only jet fighter used by the British in the Falklands fracas?

AL What form of Egyptian writing translates literally as 'sacred carving'?

SN What kind of edible fish is a 'bluefin'?

SL Which men's athletic event was won at the 1984 Olympics with a height of 2.35 metres?

286

G Which is Turkey's 'City of the Golden Horn'?

E For which organisation does actor Peter O'Brien fly?

H Who did Franklin D. Roosevelt call Uncle Joe?

AL Which common dog's name is derived from the Latin word meaning 'I trust'?

SN What name do gardeners give to lawn clippings that are left to rot into the ground as a form of fertilizer?

SL What claimed to be 'Earth's first soft drink' prior to a major slump in sales during 1989?

287

G Which European country boasts the world's largest accidental death rate?

E Which TV music programme celebrated its 40th anniversary in 1989?

H This king introduced a new dynasty onto the British throne. Who was he and what was the dynasty?

AL What do cruciverbalists fill in?

SN What colour labels did a 1989 EEC meeting suggest should be stuck on environment-friendly products?

SL How many lettered cubes are there in a *Boggle* game?

288

G Which port is reached from London via the A2?

E Which *EastEnder* character claimed to be dying in the hope that her husband would come back?

H How many children did Queen Victoria have?

AL On the front of what, does the *Spirit of Ecstasy* statuette stand?

SN What kind of creatures are divided into passerines and non-passerines?

SL What happened in the 1977 Boat Race that hasn't happened since?

289

G Which French town shares its name with the material used to make a ballerina's tutu?

E Of which hotel was Major Gowen a resident?

H Which decade saw the introduction of the incredibly slow-speed 2nd Class postal service?

AL What was the name of the parrot in *Treasure Island*?

SN To what is a pulicous animal host?

SL Who only entered three Wimbledons and won them all?

290

G Which attraction have Americans described as "The second big disappointment in marriage"?

E What was the name of Terry Wogan's chat show changed to when he had a holiday stand-in?

H Which century saw the Battle of the Alamo?

AL What type of art made Bernard Leach famous?

SN From what sort of sheep has 'pulled wool' been taken?

SL What sport's gold championships were won by Ralph Greenleaf on 19 separate occasions?

291

G Which is Florida's largest Key?

E Who played TV's *Foxy Lady*?

H Who did Roy Hattersley describe as "The Alf Garnett of British politics"?

AL Which Dickens character called the law an ass?

SN Which popular fruit is a cross between a peach and a plum?

SL How many times does a 'beamer' bounce before it zips over the batsman's head?

292

G What is the Caribbean island of St Christopher known as by its natives?

E Who went from reading the news to presenting *The Clothes Show*?

H From which London bridge was the Vatican Banker, Roberto Calvi found hanging?

AL How many ships did Helen of Troy's face launch, according to Christopher Marlowe?

SN What can be fixed by the process of mordanting?

SL Where would motorcyclists negotiate the Mountain course and the Clypse Course?

293

G What is the name of the John Lennon memorial garden in New York's Central Park?

E What does Lovejoy sell?

H Who ended his 1981 birthday conference by telling his followers to "prepare for government"?

AL How do we know that both Shakespeare and Voltaire sneezed more often than the average man?

SN Who died of cold whilst trying to freeze a chicken?

SL Which actor was runner-up in the 1979 Le Mans endurance race?

294

G How many spikes does the Statue of Liberty's crown have?

E Which of *The Young Ones* starred in *Roll Over Beethoven*?

H Which year saw Hindley and Brady tried for the Moors Murders?

AL Who wrote the famous Coronation anthem *Zadok the Priest*?

SN What two colours are most frequently mixed up in cases of colour blindness?

SL What replaced goal average when calculating Football League positions after 1974?

295

G Which river once separated Buda from Pest?

E Who was Charlie Hungerford's best known son-in-law?

H What disease became rife in Barcelona when Columbus's crew returned from their first transatlantic trip?

AL What was the name of the first *Blue Peter* dog?

SN How many sides does a dodecagon have?

SL Who was the cricketing father of the 1979 European Junior Three Day Event showjumping champion?

296

G What did environment secretary Chris Patten turn down the planned building of, at Foxley Wood, Hampshire?

E Who was *Sleeping With The Past* in a 1990 album title?

H Which American city elected David Dinkins as its first black mayor?

AL What is the better known name of Beethoven's *Symphony No. 3 in E flat*?

SN What fish becomes 'gravad lax'?

SL Off what do Olympic divers jump if they are not diving in a platform event?

297

G Which state was the original home of the Apaches?

E What was Broadway's longest running musical when it ended its run in May 1990?

H Who was the first 20th century sitting vice president of the USA to win a presidential election?

AL On whose novel did Lloyd Webber base his *Phantom of the Opera*?

SN Over what does a gnomon cast a shadow?

SL How many players are there on each team in a darts World Cup competition?

298

G Which country's capital is Godthaab?

E Who composed the music for the flop musical *Jeeves*?

H Which country's president Zia died in an aircrash?

AL What is extremely unusual about Auber's heroine from *Portici* considering that she's taking part in an opera?

SN What do paleontologists study?

SL What is the highest possible check-out in a game of darts?

299

G Which county would you visit to see a fine lady on her fine horse at Banbury Cross?

E Which comedian was cleared of eight tax fraud charges after a 23 day trial?

H Who became Prime Minister of Britain on the first occasion that 18-year-olds were allowed to vote?

AL Who flew too near to the sun?

SN What do doctors peep into with their auriscope?

SL Which player knocked England out of the 1986 World Cup and then claimed: "it was partly the hand of God"?

300

G Which continent has the most people per square mile?

E What is Rado and Ragni's best-selling musical?

H What part of J. Paul Getty III's body was sent to his mother in a box by his kidnappers?

AL What sport featured in George Bernard Shaw's novel *Cashel Byron's Profession*?

SN How many toes does an ostrich have?

SL Who won the FA Cup in 1988 without having to resort to any 'Common' tactics?

301

G Which country's equivalent to our John Bull is a woman in a red bonnet, called Marianne?

E What was James Bond's elder brother called?

H Which church was founded by John Wesley?

AL Who is Reverend W. Awdry's best-known character?

SN What is two cubed divided by two squared?

SL Which future film star won the Mr Olympia title from 1970 to 1975?

302

G What was the nickname of New York's 28th Street?

E Which pop singing son-in-law of comedian Lesley Crowther died in tragic circumstances?

H Which president was the first American to be awarded a Nobel Prize?

AL Which British painter was known as 'The Seer of Cookham'?

SN What letter and number signify America's stealth bomber which was unveiled in 1989?

SL In which city were the 1988 Winter Olympics held?

303

G From which country do true Bohemians come?

E Who sang *Looking After Number 1* and then received a knighthood for helping to look after starving millions?

H What country was Ali Agca supporting when he shot the Pope?

AL Which beginner's piece of music crops up in Borodin's *Coteletten Polka*?

SN What was the name of the supposed cure-all invented by Dr. John S. Pemberton?

SL Who was boxing's first undisputed heavyweight champion of the world?

304

G Which state did the US purchase from Spain for $5 million?

E Who used the *Yellow Pages* to track down his book on fly-fishing?

H Who left his native Ur to become the First Hebrew Patriach and the "father of a multitude of nations"?

AL Which city's bombing is central to the plot of *Slaughterhouse Five*?

SN What does an ombrophobic Mancunian fear?

SL Which Derbyshire town, famous for its water, holds an annual Shrove Tuesday football match with the goals 3 miles apart?

305

G What would you slip into Kylie Minogue's hand if she asked you for a 'middy'?

E Which British TV soap was almost called *Woodentop*?

H What was the first major Premium Bond prize worth?

AL Which author was a judge talking about when he asked "Do you think he is in need of cold, unloving rubber-insulated sex"?

SN In what subect was Elizabeth Garrett Anderson the first woman in Britain to qualify and practice?

SL What is the name of this very famous jump?

306

G What is the official language of Nigeria?

E In which of the services did Harvey Moon serve?

H What kind of establishment in Brooklyn employed Al Capone as a bouncer?

AL Who told us that the whole point about the Good Samaritan story was that he had the resources to help?

SN What is Jacques Cousteau's boat called?

SL Which games were first held at Hamilton, Ontario in 1930?

307

G What was Istanbul originally called?

E Which member of the Jackson family charted with *Escapades*?

H Which London street was the scene of a famous siege in 1911?

AL Whose picture of irises fetched a record thirty million pounds in 1987?

SN What part of a bull are you eating if the menu calls them *animelles*?

SL Which show-jumper was the BBC TV Sports Personality of 1971?

308

G Which city would you visit to see the Sikh's Golden Temple?

E Which royal princess married in a dress from *MGM* film studios?

H How did Henry VIII get rid of his first and fourth wives?

AL Which famous daughter of Lord Redesdale had a novel success with her *Christmas Pudding*?

SN Where was the world's largest radio telescope unveiled in 1957?

SL Who was sacked as England's cricket captain for irresponsible behaviour in 1988?

G Which Australian tourist attraction is said to have witnessed the death of baby Azaria Chamberlain?

E Which pop legend died three days too early to hear about the death of Groucho Marx?

H This woman gave her name to a hairstyle. What is her name?

AL Who did the 1932 Nobel Peace Prize committee have the foresight to present the 1932 literature award to, a year before his death?

SN Who was the first British test pilot to fly *Concorde*?

SL Which country will host the 1994 football World Cup Finals?

G What meal traditionally sees the Japanese dining on Miso Soup?

E What 'daring' Latin American dance became a British craze in 1910?

H On what Bill did David Alton wish to concentrate when he resigned his post as Liberal Chief Whip?

AL Which well-off stockbroker left his wife and family to take up painting in the South Seas?

SN How was the aerial raised to the necessary height for Marconi's first transatlantic wireless transmission?

SL Who scored 334 runs against England at Headingley in 1930?

G Which Middle Eastern country boasts the Bekka Valley?

E Which song has been a hit for the Communards, Harold Melvin and Thelma Houston?

H Who was the first woman to run for the vice presidency of the USA?

AL Which Chinese writer became the first author to be banned when his books were burnt in 250 B.C.?

SN Which is the only chinese year named after a feline?

SL What are the only bits of the body against which a baseball player is allowed to rub the ball?

G Which country's Condor railway station is the world's highest?

E What is the name of the girl in Simon and Garfunkel's song *America*?

H Which British MP starved himself to death in 1981?

AL Who has joint composing credits with Oscar Hammerstein for *Carmen Jones*?

SN What aid to baking was invented in 1845 by Henry Jones?

SL How can it be that both John Spencer and Ray Reardon both won the World Snooker championship in 1970?

(313)

G What is the world's largest country with no coastline?

E What at the first six words of *Get Me to the Church On Time*?

H At what royal occasion did Princess Elizabeth first meet Prince Philip?

AL Whose Streatham home displayed the motto 'My home is clean enough to be healthy and dirty enough to be happy'?

SN Who is famous for his *Birdwatch* TV programmes?

SL Which British swimmer broke the world 100 metres record at the 1989 European championships?

(314)

G Which river flows through Launceston in Australia but just misses Launceston in Cornwall?

E Which big Robin Hood role was filled by Alan Hale in three different movies?

H Of what did Sir Francis Drake die?

AL Who is this controversial author and for which novel did he win the Booker Prize in 1981?

SN What invention marks the end of the prehistoric period?

SL What number shirt did footballer Stanley Matthews always wear?

(315)

G Which US state boasts the Mount Rushmore presidential carvings?

E What were the final two words spoken by Goldie Hawn's husband as they made love, during which he died, in *Private Benjamin*?

H In which country did Charles Lindbergh complete his trans-Atlantic flight?

AL What was the first name of Italian poet Alighieri?

SN What does an ergophobic layabout fear?

SL What became the minimum age limit for female Olympic artistic gymnasts following the 1976 games?

(316)

G Which country's maps had built-in mistakes to confuse spies until 1988?

E Which film star was John Hinckley hoping to impress when he shot Ronald Reagan?

H For how many years did Edward VII rule?

AL By which war was Picasso's *Guernica* inspired?

SN Which famous black and white resident of London Zoo died in 1972?

SL Which cricketer was fined two thousand pounds for behaviour that led to an Australian Civil Court appearance?

(317)

G Which country's third largest city is Malmo?

E Which skiffle group was led by Wally Whyton?

H Which was Britain's most profitable charity in the financial year 1985-86?

AL Which *Disney* feature film character sings the song I've *Gotta Grow*?

SN Which popular pet's name means 'Good Bird' in the Aboriginal language?

SL Which team, in 1990, became the first ever to have a player sent off in the World Cup Final?

(318)

G For what do the letters U.D.I. stand?

E Who said: "When I'm good I'm very good, but when I'm bad I'm better"?

H Which Cornish site did archaeologists investigate for proof of King Arthur's existence during a 1990 dig?

AL What is the one-word title of James Joyce's 1914 collection of short stories and the name of an Irish folk group?

SN Which Sussex village was the scene of the discovery of an ancient skull in 1912 that was later proved to be a hoax?

SL Which country's embassy was entered by the SAS during an interruption to the televised snooker in 1980?

(319)

G Which river would extinguish the Statue of Liberty's torch if she fell off her stand?

E Which award winning TV series featured the 25th anniversary of the Majestics pop group?

H What high-ranking position was held by William Harrison, and later by his grandson Benjamin?

AL What does Puccini's operatic heroine Floria Tosca do for a living?

SN How many eyes does an earthworm have?

SL Which sport's first world champion was Leighton Rees?

(320)

G How many Welsh cities are there?

E What did Matt Frewer see on a bridge that gave him his stage name?

H Who beat Nelson Mandela and Jack Jones to become Chancellor of London University?

AL Whose 60th novel was called *Hickory, Dickory, Dock*?

SN Which planet's moons include Ganymede and Io?

SL Which city should a record breaking cyclist be able to reach from London in just under 4 hours 20 minutes?

(321)

G Which county would you enter first if you travelled east along the south coast of Devon?

E What kind of animal was the 'very friendly puppet called Parsley'?

H Which former actor already has a ticket to sail on the *QE2*'s millenium cruise to Egypt in the year 2000?

AL Which ballet is based on *La Belle au Bois Dormant*?

SN Of what is an androphobic woman afraid?

SL At which ground do France play their home international rugby union matches?

(322)

G What are the only parts of the Dukedom of Normandy that still belong to the Crown?

E Which TV character wrote novels under the name Mark Cain?

H Which tabloid ran the inexplicable headline 'KINNOCK POLL AXED' when labour gained hundreds of council seats in May 1990?

AL Which of his models did artist John Anthony describe as "A tough cookie"?

SN What name was later given to the nutrient factors that Sir Frederick Gowland discovered were essential for health?

SL Which city are the Ashes kept in when they are won by Australia?

(323)

G Which motorway are planes supposed to cross just before they touch down at the East Midlands Airport?

E What writing material shares its name with Russ Abbot's version of *007*?

H Which race of people were given US Citizenship under the 1924 Synder Act?

AL Who wrote *The Winslow Boy*?

SN Which English scientist contracted Chagas' Disease during his 1835 visit to South America?

SL Which sport has the significant measurement of seven feet, nine and a quarter inches?

(324)

G What is the most frequently used letter in the German language?

E Which cartoon series included Dick Dastardly before he got his own show?

H Who was the first US President to speak before the British Parliament?

AL Which Pink Floyd album title came from *The Wind in The Willows*?

SN Which gas' over-production takes most of the blame for the 'greenhouse effect'?

SL How did John White of Spurs die?

325

G Why don't cars ever run out of petrol when travelling through the Simplon Tunnel?

E Which TV series features Francesca Gonshaw and Vicki Michelle in the roles of waitresses?

H What day of the week saw the deaths of both Lincoln and Kennedy?

AL Which New York theatre was opened with a concert conducted by Tchaikovsky in 1891?

SN What is the fourth month of the Gregorian calendar?

SL What country's boxing code allows the use of the feet?

326

G Which Australian beach gets its name from an Aboriginal word meaning "noise of tumbling waves"?

E Which film actor's name was a hit for Madness?

H Who flew into Paris with the words: "Well here we are, I'm very happy"?

AL Which parts of his anatomy is the subject of Edvard Munch's *The Scream* grasping in his hands?

SN What is the female equivalent of satyriasis?

SL How many metres is the longest Olympic speed skating event?

327

G Which is the largest of New Zealand's three main Islands?

E What was the word 'Ninja' changed to in order to clean up the image of the *Teenage Mutant Ninja Turtles* for the UK?

H What year is etched on the Gold Medal of Excellence from the Paris Exhibition, depicted on a can of Campbell's soup?

AL Which mythical land was the birthplace of Aqualad?

SN Which Russian town was reported to be the site of mutant giant trees in 1989?

SL Which boxer's adopted name translates as "Praiseworthy, the most high"?

328

G Which South American country comes last alphabetically?

E This actress spent a lot of time in a giant monster's hairy grasp. Who is she and what is the name of the monster?

H Which religious group is still plodding on, even though its leaders forecast the end of the world in 1914?

AL What are the flowers if the poem begins: "I wandered lonely as a cloud"?

SN Which planet is the nearest in size to Uranus?

SL What has got stuffed in a Turkish restaurant to make dolmas?

329

G Which European capital claims to have the most fountains?

E Whose flower-power paint job was disowned by *Rolls-Royce* in 1965?

H Which standard did the USA drop in 1933?

AL To whom does Shakespeare's Horatio say: "Goodnight, sweet Prince"?

SN With what does an archer fish shoot its insect prey down?

SL Which game involves hitting the feathers of a goose with the insides of a sheep, that are named after a cat's entrails?

330

G Which Mediterranean country has a royal zoo?

E What disability is suffered by Oscar winning actress Marlee Matlin who starred in *Children of a Lesser God*?

H Which city's airport witnessed the gunning down of Benigno Aquino?

AL Who wrote *Love in a Cold Climate*?

SN Which plant is associated with the Sunday before Easter?

SL What was the name of the yacht that won the Hundred Guinea Cup in 1851?

331

G Which is the westernmost Canadian province?

E Which British rocker sang *Love Touch* the theme for the film *Legal Eagles*?

H To what kind of war did Bernard Baruch first give the name, on 16th April 1947?

AL Which Philip Roth novel had the working title *A Jewish Patient Begins His Analysis*?

SN Which is the last of a cat's senses to develop?

SL Which is the third Grand Slam event on the annual golfing calendar?

332

G In which country is Timbuktu?

E Which film saw Marlon Brando pick up his "One way ticket to Palookaville"?

H Whose death prompted President Pompidou to announce "France is widowed"?

AL What sporting term was invented by Stephen Potter?

SN What aid to decorating was invented by Norman Bleakey?

SL What was Gary Mabbutt's scoring record in the 1987 Spurs v Coventry Cup Final?

333

G Which is the world's longest mountain range?

E Who broke the record for Italy's biggest fine on an individual in 1981?

H Which Egyptian leader died eleven days before Charles de Gaulle?

AL What sport were Charters and Caldicott crazy over, in *The Lady Vanishes*?

SN Where are epidural injections given?

SL Who had the 1988 Olympic 100 metres gold taken away from him after a positive drugs test?

334

G Which county could the Queen survey if she sat on top of the flagpole at Windsor Castle?

E Which programme did detective Maggie Forbes appear in before moving to *CATS Eyes*?

H Who was the first British prime minister to visit Moscow in peace time?

AL What was relaunched in 1989 as 'The World's Greatest Book'?

SN Which famous potter was Charles Darwin's grandfather?

SL Which singing comedian was Chairman of the Rambler's Association in its 50th anniversary year?

335

G Which is the largest country in Africa?

E Which of Britain's independent radio stations has its headquarters at Brush House?

H To how many killings did Yorkshire Ripper Peter Sutcliffe plead guilty?

AL How many years of the recording contract, signed at the age of 94, did Leopold Stokowski manage to fulfil?

SN What is the opposite of diurnal?

SL Which English cricketer's first names were William Gilbert?

336

G How should you adjust your watch if you cross the International Date Line from west to east?

E Which female rocker had a *Foreign Affair* in the album chart?

H What was Mexican bandit and politician Francisco Villa's nickname?

AL Which radical British Sunday paper vanished without trace in 1987?

SN What monkey's name means 'old man of the woods'?

SL What, in 1931, became Britain's first televised horse race?

(337)

G Which famous theme park is at Anaheim, California?

E Which biblical location gave its name to a Style Council video?

H Which British prison was the scene of a major riot on April Fools' Day 1990?

AL Which appropriately named London theatre did Prince Edward go to work at after leaving the marines?

SN Which Scottish bridge cost three million pounds and the lives of 57 men?

SL Who scored Manchester United's last goal in their 92/93 Premier League-winning season?

(338)

G In which New Zealand city's harbour did the Greenpeace vessel *Rainbow Warrior* sink?

E How many discs were there in Bruce Springsteen's 1986 boxed set?

H What year saw the Liberal Party Conference decide to form a new party with the Social Democrats?

AL Which famous French painter died two days after the end of the Boxer Rebellion?

SN What anniversary did the Forth Bridge celebrate in 1990?

SL What is this famous red shirted footballer's name and how many goals did he score in the 1966 World Cup?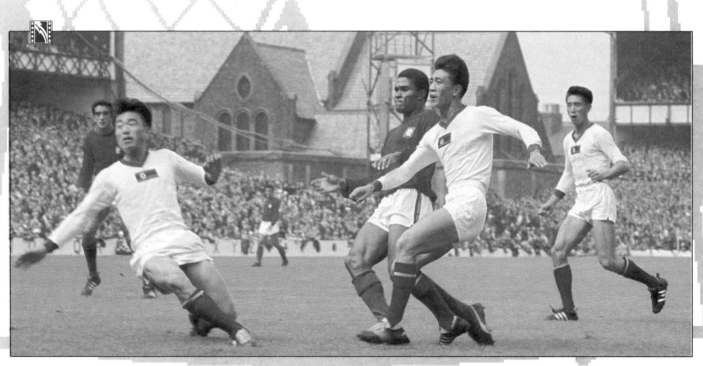

(339)

G Which US state includes the Aleutian Islands?

E What major achievement have the following got in common — *Didai Didai Dai, Diggi Loo Diggi Ley* and *Bana Bana*?

H How many people died in the bombing of the Grand Hotel, Brighton?

AL What name is given to a bell tower that isn't attached to a church?

SN How many claws does a normal house cat have?

SL Which year saw Joe Frazier take an Olympic heavyweight gold medal?

(340)

G How many stars twinkle on the New Zealand flag?

E Who called his backing band 'The Revolution'?

H Which resort hosted the 1984 Tory Party Conference?

AL Who said: "I think the essence of Judaic-teaching is very similar to *Playboy*"?

SN Which way round does a record player turntable revolve?

SL Who was the first golfer to compete against his son in a US Open golf tournament?

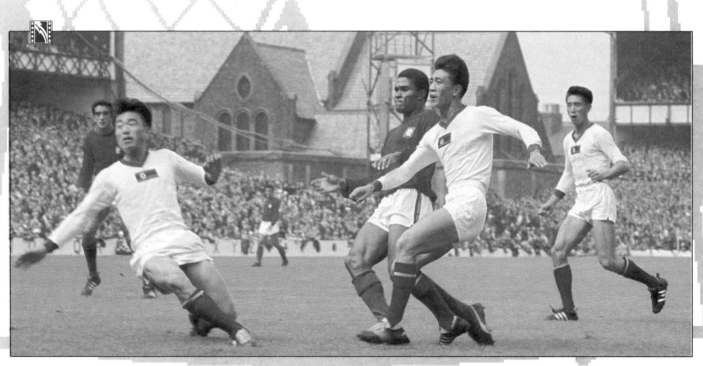

341

G How many Australian states are there?

E In which fictional suburb of Manchester would you find *Coronation Street*?

H Which member of the British Royal Family was killed in a wartime flying accident?

AL Which poet comes second only to Shakespeare when entries in the *Oxford Dictionary of Quotations* are counted?

SN Which bird is said to sing only when it is about to die?

SL Who said that politics should be kept out of sport and then took sport into politics by leading the 1989 South African cricket tour?

342

G What type of cheese is traditionally made in the Yorkshire Dales villages of Hawes and Aysgarth?

E Which song did Carl Perkins claim to have written on a potato sack?

H Which Australian prime minister drowned in 1967?

AL Which ballet features a prince who falls in love with a bird (of the feathered variety)?

SN What kind of animals are avifauna?

SL Who was the first cricketer to play in a Test Match after receiving a knighthood?

343

G Which Spanish province includes the Costa del Sol?

E Which appropriately named band had a 1990 dancefloor smash with *Never Penetrate*?

H On what was millionaire John Jacob Astor standing at the time of his death?

AL In the form of what did Anthony Cavendish publish his MI6 memoirs to circumvent the ban on such publications?

SN What popular garden plant is nicknamed the 'Butterfly Bush'?

SL Which golf course is known as 'The Old Lady'?

344

G Which of the following is not entitled to enter the Eurovision Song Contest — Tunisia, Libya, Kenya or Israel?

E Which member of the Stranglers was romantically linked with Hazel O'Connor?

H What did the first Labour leader Keir Hardie do for a living before taking up politics?

AL By what name was American painter Anna Mary Moses better known?

SN Of what is walleyed the opposite?

SL Who is the President of the British Olympic Association?

345

G Which New York location is the home of the American Cleopatra's Needle?

E Who wrote *The South Bank Show's* signature tune?

H Who didn't go to Charles and Diana's wedding because she thought it should be for younger people?

AL Which classic novel is narrated by Jim Hawkins?

SN By what name is the anti morning-sickness drug Sistaval better known?

SL Who was the first player to top 5000 runs in one day cricket internationals?

346

G Which is the only US city that looks southward into Canada?

E Who was the zoo keeper in *Animal Magic*?

H Whose 400 pairs of shoes made headlines in 1986?

AL Which bit of a frog went into the *Macbeth* witches' potion?

SN What kind of precious stone is the *Star of Delhi*?

SL Which English cricket captain has the appropriate initials M.C.C.

347

G Which country is famous for supplying flags of convenience to ships from other countries?

E Who were the second Swedish group to have a UK number 1 hit?

H Which of its own MPs did Labour disown in 1987 due to his views on troops in Northern Ireland?

AL Whose first opera was *Nabucco* and last *Falstaff*?

SN How many rivets (in round millions) are there in the Forth Bridge?

SL Who was lost on Everest with George Mallory?

348

G Which country's capital is P'yongyang?

E Which 1975 blockbuster of a movie centred around the fishy goings on in the township of Amity?

H Which ship made headlines when it was sent to Bremerhaven for a major 1983 refit?

AL What is Bottom's first name in *A Midsummer Night's Dream*?

SN Which two scientists' laboratory notebooks were checked for radiation prior to being auctioned in 1984?

SL What five-letter word is used by collectors to describe the highest quality of coin to be minted?

349

G Which Swiss city is said to have got its name because thousands of bears were killed there on the day of foundation?

E What was Kermit the Frog's nephew called?

H How many children did Henry VIII's children have between them?

AL Which band's album covers made photographer Robert Freeman famous?

SN What sort of people have an appetite for anthropophagy?

SL How many players should be on the rink at any one time in a game of ice hockey?

350

G Which Mediterranean holiday country is served by Monastir Airport?

E Which coastal town had 'Dad's Army' for its wartime defence?

H Who was the first American president to be born in a hospital?

AL Which new publication was voted Britain's newspaper of the year in 1986?

SN What controversial electrical device intended to end controversies was invented by John Augustus Larson in 1921?

SL What has a 'maiden' racehorse never done?

351

G What country can be seen from the top of the Blackpool Tower on a perfectly clear day?

E Who was TV's *District Nurse*?

H Who turned down the offer of Israel's presidency in 1948?

AL Where is this man buried?

SN What key is to the left of the K on a standard QWERTY typewriter?

SL How many times were the Olympic Games held in the 1970s?

352

G Which South American country would have to grant you permission if you wished to take home an Easter Island statue?

E What is the name of Lesley Grantham's *Paradise Club* character?

H How many people were killed when the *Rainbow Warrior* was blown up?

AL Which book by Frances Hodgson Burnett tells of little Cedric who inherits a title and a fortune?

SN What are dromophobiacs frightened of crossing?

SL Which Olympic swimming event could feature a barracuda back pike somersault?

G Which North African country has a plain green rectangle for a flag?

E Which TV comedy series features the Tates and the Campbells?

H Who got a loan from the US Government to return to America in 1962 partly because he thought Russian winters were making him bald?

AL Which crime-fighter's parents were shot dead by Joel Chill?

SN Which was the first country to have sent two women into space?

SL Which professional golfer noted: "There are no rich Mexicans, they get some money, they call themselves Spanish!"?

G What is the official language of Sri Lanka?

E Which poet did Bob Dylan say he didn't name himself after, even if most books say that he did?

H What commodity shortage was the single main factor for keeping most of the world's cars off the roads during World War II?

AL Which cartoonist's works were the inspiration for the animators of Pink Floyd's *The Wall*?

SN What is the common name for the teenage affliction 'Comedo'?

SL What was Mallory's three-word reply when asked why he wanted to climb Everest?

G Which holiday isle is the southernmost point of continental USA?

E Which right-wing, former Labour peer became the controversial deputy head of the *IBA* in 1989?

H Which religious leader and his followers committed what he called: "An act of revolutionary suicide", in 1978?

AL What is the secret identity of Kathy Kane?

SN Which country is home to the largest number of bald eagles, the USA's national symbol?

SL Which is the only horse to have won the Derby by ten lengths?

G Which tiny Pacific island's main settlement is Adamstown, near Bounty Bay?

E Which Don McLean hit was spread across both sides of the original single?

H Who is the only person to have held ten different British government posts?

AL To whom is A.A. Milne's *When We Were Very Young* dedicated?

SN What is the name given to a tube used for taking fluid from the human body?

SL What sport features in *Jack High*?

G Which large island lies just a few miles south of Corsica?

E Where was Daniel's plane heading for when he left Elton John?

H Who was the first US president sworn in on national television?

AL What does the Koran name as the forbidden fruit?

SN What is the effect of an antipyretic drug?

SL Which TV cricket commentator was once a Liberal Party candidate?

G What was Sri Lanka's main crop prior to tea?

E Which film's posters advised "Fasten your seat belts! For a ride you'll never forget"?

H What did Leofric, the Earl of Mercia's wife have between her legs when she made her most famous historical gesture?

AL Who was jilted on her wedding day in *Great Expectations*?

SN What kind of television set would a chromophobe prefer?

SL How much weight loss (in pounds) are jump jockeys allowed to show during a race?

G Which European country would lose its independence if there was no heir to its throne?

E Which saint's story was told in the film *Brother Sun, Sister Moon*?

H Where would you find almost 3000 standing stones at Northern France's equivalent of Stonehenge?

AL Which Robert Louis Stevenson character murdered Sir Danvers Carew?

SN What bottled liquid are Japan's pampered Kobe cattle regularly fed?

SL Who won the Cricket Writers' Club *Young Cricketer of the Year* competition in 1977?

G Which European country has no single person as its head of state?

E What should you never give a sucker according to a 1941 W. C. Fields film title?

H How many thousand people are said to have died when the bomb was dropped on Hiroshima?

AL Which Hugh Loftin character lived at Puddleby-on-Marsh and was taught by a parrot called Polynesia?

SN What bit of your anatomy would your lover lift up if he or she wanted to examine your septum linguae?

SL Which Derby was won by Patricia's Hope?

361

G Which two countries look at each other across the world's shortest national frontier?

E Which 1940 animated film included Disney's theme song *When You Wish Upon A Star*?

H Which was the world's largest exporter of goods in 1987?

AL How many stories are there in Boccaccio's *Decameron*?

SN Which explorer introduced the pig to the North American continent?

SL Who achieved the first ever Olympic gymnastic score of 10 at the 1976 Montreal games?

362

G In which state is Washington D.C.?

E Who played Ralph 'Papa' Thorson in his final film role?

H This man is famous for getting lost where?

AL Which Dickens character's stepfather was Edward Murdstone?

SN Which rodent follows on after the Chinese Year of the Pig?

SL Who is the only US boxer to have both won and lost his world title outside the USA?

363

G Which eastern country claims the highest per annum, per capita consumption of alcohol?

E Which character is associated with the song *Bibbidy-Bobbidy-Boo* in Walt Disney's *Cinderella*?

H Which two years saw Arthur Scargill leading Britain's famous Miners' Strike?

AL Which Thomas Mann book sees a middle-aged German composer die of cholera in an Italian tourist city?

SN Did Einstein ever win a Nobel Prize?

SL Who, in 1979, became the first World Indoor Bowls Champion?

364

G What kind of pasta has a name that means 'little worms'?

E Which 1957 US hit for the Rays was a 1990 UK smash for Cliff Richard?

H Who was Gerald Ford speaking of when he said: "He doesn't dye his hair, he is just prematurely orange"?

AL For what were Vile and Cobb famous?

SN Which branch of chemistry is concerned wholly with carbon compounds?

SL Who was called 'The new Jesse Owens' after his 1984 Olympic performance?

365

G How many million square miles of the Earth's surface are covered by the Pacific Ocean — 52, 65, 76 or 88?

E Which company produces the *Flying V* guitar, a favourite of Jimi Hendrix?

H What nationality invented the Frankfurter?

AL What is seen on 'St. Veronica's Handkerchief'?

SN Which is longer, a light year or a parsec?

SL What is the shortest Olympic race in which lane changes are allowed?

366

G Which European city is always listed first in an A to Z gazetteer?

E Which Elvis Presley single was the first ever to break in to the UK charts at number one?

H Which king's *Times* obituary began: "There can hardly be a wet eye in the kingdom for this debauched monarch"?

AL What name is given to diluted clay which can be trailed on a pot to give decoration?

SN What sign of the zodiac is depicted by this animal?

SL What did Ronald Reagan describe as: "A game in which you can feel a clean hatred for your opponent"?

367

G In which county is most of the Duchy of Cornwall?

E Who is the only person to have had eight simultaneous records in the UK top 30?

H Which news reading vicar's daughter turned down fifty thousand pounds to appear nude in *Penthouse*?

AL Who is seen in his bath in Jacques-Louis David's most famous painting?

SN What action does the average cow perform for 75 per cent of its day?

SL What brand number is printed on the label of *Jack Daniel's* whiskey?

368

G Which European country offers holidays in paradors?

E Which pop star's mother and father had bit-parts in the film *Loving You*?

H How many years after the end of food rationing in Great Britain was the *McDonald's* hamburger launched in the States?

AL What type of decorative item is a kilim?

SN Which has more bones, the ankle or the wrist?

SL What is traditionally served stuck in the neck of a bottle of Mexican *Corona* beer?

369

G Which US state's official song is *Home, Home On the Range*?

E What was Elvis Presley's first UK number one hit single?

H What coin was valued at six shillings until 1849 when its value dropped to two?

AL Which composer won a British Film Academy Award for his score for *The French Lieutenant's Woman*?

SN What did the ancient Romans call the eighth day following the Nones?

SL What turns pineapple juice and lime juice into a 'Matador'?

370

G Which flower is the national symbol of India?

E Who did Ivan Vaughan introduce to John Lennon at Woolton Parish Church Fete in 1957?

H Which famous funnyman kept a German bank account throughout the war "Just in case the little bastard wins"?

AL Which Alice Walker Pulitzer Prize winner became a Whoopi Goldberg film directed by Steven Spielberg?

SN What four-letter word describes an expensive form of deep red corundum?

SL Who reached the final every time he competed at Wimbledon from 1959 to 1969?

371

G Which country's capital is Tirana?

E What name did John Beverly adopt when he shot to fame as a Sex Pistol?

H Who is said to have joined Ethelred the Unready and his wife in bed on their wedding night?

AL Which American artist directed the film *Chelsea Girl*?

SN How many volts are there in an A.A. battery?

SL What do you race if you have OBs and YBs?

372

G What do one hundred Austrian groschen make?

E What year saw Elvis Presley enter the army?

H How did the Crusaders make the bodies of their dead comrades light enough to bring home for burial?

AL How did a 1661 issue of the Bible word one of the Ten Commandments, to become known as *The Wicked Bible*?

SN What revolutionary kind of door did Theophilus Van Kannel invent in 1885?

SL What achievement wins the annual Golden Boot for footballers?

373

G Which country was the setting for *The Killing Fields*?

E In which *Coronation Street* building did Martha Longhurst die?

H For what is ECU an abbreviation?

AL What is the meaning of the Order of the Garter motto: "Honi Soit qui Mal y Pense"?

SN What do people in TV commercials call 'seborrhoea', when they cruelly draw attention to the fact that someone's a sufferer?

SL Who got back to a home that gales had blown the roof off, after winning the 1982 world darts championship?

374

G What is the name of the house in Memphis that Mrs Ruth Brown-Moore sold to a singer on 19th March, 1957?

E Which D. J. got his big break by standing in for Kenny Everett when he was off work sick?

H Who was leader of the Labour Party immediately prior to Michael Foot?

AL What is the meaning of the English Royal motto "Dieu et Mon Droit"?

SN Which bit does a firefly flash?

SL Who, in 1956, won the first track Olympic gold for Britain since 1932, and became chairman of the British Orienteering Federation in 1967?

375

G Which country was known as Blighty during the First World War?

E Which TV series included characters called Doris and Shorofsky?

H Which war included the Battle of Shiloh?

AL Which word meaning chaos was first used by Milton in *Paradise Lost*?

SN What violet-blue variety of quartz was once said to prevent drunkenness?

SL Who was the first British boxer to win the world featherweight title?

376

G Which London palace is said to be haunted by Anne Boleyn, Katherine Howard and Jane Seymour?

E Which song by the Goons was a hit in 1956 and in 1973?

H Which organization had Len Murray as its General Secretary from 1973 to 1984?

AL Who is the subject of an alleged murder in the book *In God's Name*?

SN What vitamin in liver was found to be dangerous to pregnant women if digested in quantity?

SL What does the J stand for in J.P.R. Williams' name?

377

G Which West Texas town shares its name with one of the Muppets?

E This actress has played in films opposite Elvis Presley, Pat Boone and The Who. Who is she?

H Which US vice president resigned in 1973?

AL To reach up to what was the Tower of Babel built?

SN Which Italian physicist went as a delegate to the Paris peace conference following World War I?

SL With which baseball team did Joe di Maggio spend most of his career?

378

G Who is your landlord if you are locked up in Dartmoor Prison?

E Which Radio 1 D.J. interviewed John Lennon two days before his assassination?

H Who was being tried when a policeman, who had dressed as a transvestite called Amanda, gave evidence?

AL Which work by Shakespeare is known as *The Scottish Play*?

SN What is the more childish name for antirrhinums?

SL Which British athelete broke the world mile record in Oslo in July 1985?

379

G Which London Palace's guard is changed at 11.15 each morning?

E Which disc jockey took over the *Any Questions* chair from Freddy Grisewood?

H Which city was Terry Waite staying in at the time of his disappearance?

AL What is the proper name of the theatre often known simply as Drury Lane?

SN What would you be doing at Wimbledon if you had a Cambridge Rival in your mouth?

SL Who won two women's track medals for Britain at the 1984 Olympics?

380

G Which part of French Guiana was famous as a penal colony?

E Which trumpet player is the A in A & M Records if Jerry Moss is the M?

H Who was second choice for rebuilding St. Paul's after the Great Fire, and had two sets of plans turned down?

AL Where in the Tate Gallery can you feast your eyes on Rex Whistler's most famous murals?

SN Which continent is the natural habitat of the popular spider plant?

SL Which American vice-president officially opened the 1960 Winter Olympics?

381

G What is the origin of the majority of Fiji's population?

E Which member of Herd and Humble Pie became known as 'The Face of 1968'?

H Which European country didn't give its women the vote until 1944?

AL Whose paintings were once described as "Oodles of Goddesses without any bodices"?

SN What number was given to *Boeing's* first commercial jet airliner?

SL What is your sport if your balls are scrutinized with an Overall Distance Standard?

382

G What do Americans call an estate agent?

E Which was the first British music paper to run a top 50 singles chart?

H What popular drink was first brewed for Americans by Englishman Richard Blechynden in the heat of the 1904 St. Louis World's Fair?

AL How is the surname FEATHERSTONEHAUGH pronounced?

SN What did the Italian manufaturer of this car specialise in before venturing into sportscar making?

SL Why was a new FA Cup made for the 1896 Cup Final?

383

G Which country's Pedaung women are famous for the way in which they stretch their necks with metal rings?

E Which movie finds Marty McFly being fancied by his own mother in the year 1955?

H Which political party placed its lectern to one side of the stage, rather than in the centre for its 1990 conference?

AL What was 'An Unsuitable Job For A Woman' in P.D. James's *An Unsuitable Job For A Woman*?

SN What do dendrologists study?

SL What is the playing surface for the French Open tennis tournament?

384

G Which city would you head for if you were given a grant to study in the place that the Romans called Granta?

E Which Bobby Charles record was covered by Bill Haley and is still used as a means of farewell?

H Who was Churchill's Deputy Prime Minister during the Second World War?

AL Which city was the setting for *A Streetcar Named Desire*?

SN What name is given to the process of determining the amount of individual metals in ore samples?

SL Which university played in the second and third FA Cup Finals?

385

G What would be the next place you came to if you travelled due west from Cape Horn?

E Which other actress's surname is mentioned in the Kim Carnes hit *Bette Davis Eyes*?

H What luxury commodity established John Jacob Astor's fortune?

AL Which literary picture was painted by Basil Hallward?

SN With what natural substance are violin bows strung?

SL What did Lt. Creswel break during the very first Cup Final, to get his name in the record books?

386

G Which country is known as the 'Cockpit of Europe'?

E Which famous radio role was filled by both Ellis Powell and Jessie Matthews?

H Which prime minister was in office during most of the Suffragette problems?

AL In what season does Shakespeare's *A Midsummer Night's Dream* take place?

SN What compound makes carrots orange?

SL Who had won most of the Manchester City v United derby matches up to the end of the 1989-90 season?

387

G What should go round a city that has 'Chester' at the end of its name?

E After what precious stone did Mick Jagger name his daughter?

H What was Prime Minister Herbert Henry Asquith's political party?

AL Who was the last to stab Caesar in Shakespeare's *Julius Caesar*?

SN Which is bigger a gene or a chromosome?

SL Which team had won most of the Everton v Liverpool derby matches up to the end of the 1989-90 season?

388

G Why does Canada's Wood Buffalo National Park feature in record books?

E Which animated Spielberg movie features Russian mice called the Mousekowites?

H What was the full name of Patty Hearst's kidnappers, the SLA?

AL What was 'Hobson's choice'?

SN What do bruxomaniacs grind together?

SL Which country won the gold medal in the 1984 Los Angeles Olympics demonstration sport of baseball?

389

G Which country must you visit to see the geyser that was originally called 'Geyser'?

E What was the sequel to *Alien* called?

H What general term describes the age between the Stone Age and the Iron Age?

AL Which moor is the setting for *Lorna Doone*?

SN Of what can a woman have more than one in a polyandric society?

SL What is the modern name for a golfer's ten-iron?

390

G Which Mediterranean island boasts the famous Blue Grotto?

E Which aircraft is named in the title of the film *Airport '80*?

H Who was President of the USA when the Wall Street Crash swept up half the country's savings?

AL Which Dickens character was Mr. Murdstone's stepson?

SN How many kilometres are there in a megametre?

SL How many horses do you back in a *Round Robin*?

391

G Which river is crossed by toll bridge to reach Cornwall from Devon?

E Which leggy French dance team was founded by Margaret Kelly?

H What reed did the ancient Egyptians make into a type of paper?

AL What was the relationship between King Arthur and Morgan Le Fey?

SN What do scatologists probe into during their studies?

SL Which sport were women in Australia banned from watching until 1908?

392

G What is the official language of Liechtenstein?

E Which song by Chicory Tip was the first UK number one to feature a synthesizer solo?

H As what is Kublai Khan's capital 'Cambaluc' now better known?

AL Which artist was played by Kirk Douglas in the film *Lust For Life*?

SN What medical condition are you suffering from if you have an inflamed bursa?

SL Which country topped the medals table in the 1988 Olympic Games?

(393)

G Of what did the town of Raudhatain in Kuwait start to pump out 5 million gallons a day, after a valuable 1961 discovery?

E To which folk singer was the Crosby, Stills and Nash song *Suite: Judy Blue Eyes* dedicated?

H Who is known as 'Father of the House of Commons' thanks to his inviting the first commoners to become MPs?

AL Which Yorkshire village is a place of pilgrimage for fans of these 3 sisters?

SN On which tree do elderberries grow?

SL Is there such an Olympic event as synchronized swimming for one person?

(394)

G On which river estuary does Swansea stand?

E What are the first names of the musical duo Hodges and Peacock?

H Which Kennedy died in the same year as Martin Luther King?

AL Which Shakespeare play finds Viola disguised as Cesario?

SN Which sea-going mammal is also known as the 'cachalot'?

SL Which London rugby club included J.P.R. Williams in its squad?

(395)

G Which town's Peterhouse College was founded in 1284?

E Which famous black comedy actor was brought up in a brothel?

H What year saw the launch of *Sputnik I*?

AL Which musical was based on the play *The Matchmaker*?

SN Which animal has heart-shaped hoof prints and excrement that smells of violets?

SL Who was the only British World Heavyweight Boxing champion?

(396)

G On which African country is Bulawayo?

E Which TV sci-fi crew had an enemy called Travis?

H How old was Diana Spencer when her title changed from Lady to Princess?

AL What colour is the tablecloth in Leonardo's *The Last Supper*?

SN What effect does adrenaline have on the heart rate?

SL Which British sprinter was born on 1st April, 1960 in Jamaica?

397

G Which is the world's largest museum?

E Which actor went from *EastEnders* to *The Paradise Club*?

H Who was ice-picked to death by Ramon Mercader, acting under orders from Stalin?

AL Whose *The Simiarillion* was published posthumously?

SN What was Johann Nepomuk Maelzel's scientific gift to the world of music?

SL What pole vault height was first cleared by Javier Sotomayor of Cuba?

398

G Which body of water caresses Brest's bobbing maidens?

E Who hosts *Fun House*?

H Of which country was Kenneth Kaunda the first president?

AL Which literary character sold her sawmills to Ashley Wilkes?

SN What name is given to permanently frozen sub-soil?

SL Who had notched up a record number of National Hunt wins by the end of the 1989 season?

399

G What do the French call their police?

E Who played Carter in *The Sweeney*?

H How many US presidents were assassinated during Queen Victoria's reign?

AL What is the name of the pub in *Treasure Island*?

SN Of what other metal can sterling silver contain 7.5 percent?

SL What is the American name for draughts?

400

G Which Australian state capital was named after a British prime minister?

E Where does Granny Dryden live?

H Which US city was named after the first president of the Republic of Texas?

AL Which novelist's works included *Henrietta Temple* and *Venetia* prior to his becoming Prime Minister in 1868?

SN Of what does the average male body have 5 million?

SL What is the surname of the ex-Welsh International rugby player with the fornames John Peter Rhys?

401

G Which country are you in if you've just reached the joining of the Wang and Ping rivers at Tak?

E What is the relationship between Oliver Reed and sports reporter Simon Reed?

H Which annual American holiday celebrates the lean harvest of 1621?

AL Whose *Pieta* is the only one of his works known to carry his signature?

SN Which part of the body is mentioned in both of Art Garfunkel's solo number one hits?

SL Who qualified for the 1990 World Cup finals after a 0-0 draw with Poland?

402

G Which clock-making city is served by Cointrin Airport?

E Which TV character's catchphrase is "Don't be a plonker all your life"?

H What year saw the commencement of the building of the Berlin Wall?

AL Who did *Private Eye* call Captain Bob?

SN What kind of bank cools down its deposits to minus 196.5 degrees Centigrade?

SL Which colour snooker ball has the lowest score value?

403

G What is the highest mountain on the North American continent?

E What role did Robert Stack fill in *The Untouchables*?

H How many of Henry VIII's wives were beheaded?

AL Which city saw Jekyll go to Hyde?

SN For which field of study did the National Bank of Sweden institute a Nobel Prize in 1968?

SL How many players take part in a Gaelic Football match?

404

G Which country claims the most followers of Mohammed?

E Which film features a cartoonist, an architect, an actor and a very young child?

H Which leader joked: "If you think I'm a radical, wait until you see my little brother Raul"?

AL Which character in a Browning poem wears "a queer long coat" that is "half yellow and half red"?

SN What do most doctors have hanging in their surgery that is most likely of the Snellen variety?

SL Which football club is known as the Canaries?

405

G Which country boasts Wood Buffalo National Park; the world's largest?

E What was Chris de Burgh's colourful 'number one' single when Madonna was topping the album chart with *True Blue*?

H What did the Saxe-Coburg-Gothas diplomatically change their name to in 1917?

AL What does the salesman sell in *Death of a Salesman*?

SN What colour are the seeds of a pawpaw?

SL Where should the marker be placed on the green in relation to the golf ball if you wish to move it?

406

G Which is the largest Indonesian island?

E Which TV superhero attends 'Shuster University'?

H Which American made his last public speech on 10th April 1865?

AL Which trio "sailed on a river of crystal light into a sea of dee"?

SN How many degrees of longitude are covered by each of the earth's timezones?

SL Which country was awarded the America's cup in 1989 following a supreme court ruling?

407

G Which is Australia's most northerly city?

E What did Israel's minister of science try to ban in 1987 as "an insult to our national intelligence"?

H What was the name of the WPC murdered by Libyans in London's St. James's Square?

AL What word did Bizet use to describe *The Toreador* song from *Carmen*?

SN How many planets are bigger than earth?

SL Who did Henry Cooper beat to win his first British heavyweight title in 1959?

408

G This famous cathedral is found in a city the name of which was also a hit for Ultravox. What is the city's name?

E Which male animal provided Paul McCartney with the title for his second solo album?

H Who set off with his father and uncle to visit the court of Kublai Khan in 1271?

AL Who was painter Ben Nicholson's famous sculptress wife?

SN Which cubit is longest — the Biblical, Greek or Roman?

SL Which British golfer won the 1989 US Masters Championship?

409

G Which country has the world's largest Jewish population?

E Which popular 1958 film told the story of Gladys Aylward, the English girl who became a missionary in China?

H Which country would you visit to see the ancient Lion Gate at Mycenae?

AL What did Fungus the Bogeyman and his wife Mildew call their son?

SN Which part of the body consumes 40 per cent of the blood's oxygen?

SL Who was the first British woman to swim the 400 metres medley in less than 5 minutes?

410

G Which country is registered as having the world's largest merchant navy?

E Who co-starred with Rachel Ward in the 1984 thriller *Against All Odds*?

H Which leader had a great horse called Bucephalus, that no one else could ride?

AL Who kills Archdeacon Frollo in *The Hunchback of Notre Dame*?

SN On what do you constantly chew if you are suffering from autophagia?

SL What was the sport of Tommy Simpson, the 1965 BBC Sports Personality of the Year?

411

G Which two Australian states are separated by the Bass Strait?

E What kind of music was popularized in the UK by Harry Belafonte and the Tarriers?

H Which bald English queen packed out her sunken cheeks with silk handkerchiefs?

AL Which Shakespeare play was the basis for the rock opera *Catch My Soul*?

SN Which order of mammals is made up of prosimians and anthropoids?

SL What describes a ten-second lawn in a game of bowls – slow or fast?

412

G Which city's international airport is Canada's busiest?

E Which legendary hero has provided an acting role for Diane Cilento's husband Sean Connery, and son Jason Connery?

H Which member of the Royal Family has sisters called Jane and Sarah?

AL Which nursery rhyme character was based on the rather rotund Richard III?

SN What type of animal is 'Canis Familiaris'?

SL Who was the first player to complete the tennis 'Grand Slam'?

413

G To which island off their own coast are US citizens not allowed to travel?

E Which Hollywood superstar had a cameo role as the Doctor in *Tommy*?

H How old was Princess Anne when she became Princess Royal?

AL Which Gilbert and Sullivan opera is set in a law court?

SN What kind of vegetable is a Musselburgh?

SL Which racecourse features the Rowley Mile?

414

G Which was the first British town with a motorway by-pass?

E Which war was the setting for *Wings*?

H How many former prime ministers were alive when Harold Macmillan died?

AL What did St. Paul advise drinking instead of water "for thy stomach's sake"?

SN Which flower originally came from Turkey and was given the name "Turk's Hat"?

SL How many pins are used in a game of traditional West Country skittles?

415

G Of what has Birmingham got 22 miles more than Venice?

E Who was the man who got shot by John Wayne in the role of Ton Doniphon?

H Which century saw the last legal burning of a witch in England?

AL What does a homonym have?

SN What is the normal human body temperature in degrees Celsius?

SL Who is normally only around at Christmas but managed to win the 1964 Derby?

416

G What is the largest island in the Indian Ocean?

E Which James Bond baddie had Oddjob as his bodyguard?

H Which highly paid group of people received no salary at all until 1911?

AL What were the names of Helen of Troy's twin sons?

SN What do cordwainers make?

SL Which player will be forever connected with the 1953 FA Cup Final?

417

G Which is the Islamic world's most heavily populated city?

E With which band did Peter Cetera sing prior to solo success with *The Glory of Love*?

H Which saint was the first Archbishop of Canterbury?

AL Which institution published its last *Index of Forbidden Books* in 1966?

SN Which rock movie took its title from the common name for a lumbar puncture?

SL Which English ladies' college town shares its name with an Adelaide racecourse?

418

G Who traditionally cries all the way through a Finnish wedding?

E What female name can be added to Muffins or Vandellas to become the name of a pop group?

H For what did the initials BEF stand during both world wars?

AL Which novel finds James Bond in the suicide gardens of Dr. Shatterhand?

SN Which is the closest planet with a moon to the sun?

SL How many fingers are used in the Boy Scout salute?

419

G Which body of water forms Turkey's northern border?

E What subject do Hudson and Halls turn into television entertainment?

H Who is this man and where did he spend the last days of his life?

AL Which area of Spain is mentioned in the first line of *Don Quixote*?

SN What type of weapons did George Bush propose to "banish from the face of the earth" during 1989?

SL What kind of tree is pictured on a *Kahlua* coffee liqueur label?

420

G Which city is the most northerly stop for the Marrakesh Express?

E Which long-running TV series featured a wartime unit with the number 4077?

H What year saw the abolition of the death penalty for murder in Britain?

AL Which major modern artist died in 1987 in New York after a gall bladder operation?

SN How many incisor teeth does a fully-grown elephant have?

SL Where do pitchers limber up before joining a baseball match?

421

G This flower is the national flower of Austria. What is it?

E Which *Coronation Street* actress went on to *Constant Hot Water*?

H Which king said: "Let not poor Nelly starve" shortly before his death?

AL How many sons did William Shakespeare's father have?

SN What would be the main vitamin benefit gained by eating a polar bear's liver?

SL In which motor race does Paul Newman take part, at the close of the film *Winning*?

422

G Who traditionally found whom on the Juan Fernandez islands?

E What was Emily's surname before she became a Bishop?

H Who made a plea from jail for his wife to get rid of her 'Football Team' after they were accused of several murders?

AL Whose painting *The Potato Eaters* was stolen in 1988?

SN What did a New Zealand museum worker do with one of the world's two remaining Moa eggs in 1990?

SL How many 'downs' does each team have, to travel ten yards in American Football?

423

G Which Asian peak is named after a former British Surveyor General in India?

E Which TV quiz show has been hosted by Julian Pettifer and Sarah Kennedy?

H Which former film star expressed his happiness at having had "this affair with Princess David"?

AL How many legs does a 'Triffid' have?

SN What are *Resolution, Renown* and *Repulse*?

SL Which Carling Premiership team plays in red or green and yellow or black?

424

G Which country consists of the Jutland Peninsula and several islands?

E Which early film star was known as the 'Million Dollar Mermaid'?

H What female name did John F. Kennedy give to his presidential campaign aircraft?

AL What does the dawn come up like on *The Road to Mandalay*?

SN What animal is called a 'teg' at the age of two?

SL What is a 'Liverpool Kiss'?

425

G Which island saw the first *Club Med?*

E Who was a chart topper for Toni Basil?

H Which two US presidents received subpoenas to testify in the Oliver North case?

AL What was the name of the Hunchback of Notre Dame's girlfriend?

SN Where do Arctic Terns migrate to?

SL How long do fighters get to recover between each round of professional boxing?

426

G What is the name of Bermuda's biggest island?

E Who was the first film producer to appear on a US postage stamp?

H What was the irreverent nickname for this British monarch?

AL Which day's "child has far to go"?

SN Which mouse is a protected species in Britain?

SL Who said: "The medals weigh more than I thought. It was hard to stand up straight with them round my neck"?

427

G Which Kentish cathedral's central tower is called Bell Harry?

E Which famous reggae singer's father was an English army captain?

H Which country became a republic when it withdrew from the Commonwealth in 1961?

AL What is the Irish equivalent of the bagpipes in which the bellows are squeezed under the arm?

SN Which drug did John F. Kennedy take for backache during the last 15 years of his life?

SL How many substitutes is each team allowed in a game of American Football — 2, 12, 22 or 32?

428

G What name is given to a charcoal-heated Russian tea-urn?

E Where was the club that was a 1990 hit for Elton John?

H In front of which Washington hotel was Ronald Reagan shot in 1981?

AL Which Jane Fonda film was based on a comic strip by Jean Claude Forest?

SN What is injected to regulate diabetes?

SL Who is the only player to have scored 38 goals in FA Cup matches?

429

G Which English county grows more potatoes than any other?

E Which member of the Royal Family devised the royal version of *It's A Knockout*?

H What name is shared by the philosopher who became Lord Chancellor in 1628, and an important modern British painter?

AL Which Shakespeare play title gave David Essex a hit record?

SN What is LOX to an astronaut if it isn't smoked salmon?

SL What was the surname of the 1878 Cup Final referee, that has often been attached to referees since?

430

G Which country includes the region of Assam?

E Which classic Irving Berlin dance number begins "If you're blue and you don't know where to go..."?

H Who murdered Police Officer Tippit in Dallas on 22nd November 1963?

AL Which Florentine painter, and Dominican friar was described by Ruskin as "not an artist properly so-called, but an inspired saint"?

SN Of which flower family is asparagus a member?

SL Which British athlete won the Olympic 1500m gold medal twice?

431

G Which country did Winston Churchill call 'The sleeping giant'?

E Which actor agreed to play a tramp in *Coronation Street* but had to back out due to filming commitments?

H With which Henry did Thomas á Becket have his fatal arguments?

AL Who sold the ring to the Owl and the Pussycat?

SN Which antipodean bird's eggs are incubated by the male?

SL What did Blackburn Rovers do immediately before the 1883 Cup Final that no other cup Final team had done before?

432

G What colour robes do Benedictine monks wear?

E Who paid Sam Phillips four dollars to record *My Happiness* for his mum's birthday in 1953?

H Who shared the 1978 Nobel Peace Prize with Menachem Begin?

AL Who married the Owl and the Pussycat?

SN What colour is a St. Bernard's nose?

SL Which Lancashire soccer team was the first to achieve the League and Cup double?

433

G Why won't the Spaniards sing their national anthem if they reach the final of the 1994 World Cup?

E Who directed, produced, co-wrote and starred in *Yentl?*

H Which century saw Ancient Rome at its absolute peak?

AL Which of his novels did George Orwell intend calling *The Last Man In Europe*?

SN What is a 'Plymouth Rock' if it is breathing?

SL Which decade first saw motor races averaging in excess of 80mph?

434

G Which European country has the smallest population?

E Which animator went from the Pink Panther to Roger Rabbit?

H Which century saw the banning of the rank of samurai in Japan?

AL Which Henry Fielding hero married Sophia Western?

SN Does an average red-blooded male really have more red blood cells than the average female?

SL Which sport put Udo Beyer in the world record lists?

435

G What is the official language of Haiti?

E Which 1984 movie saw the renewal of Olivia Newton John and John Travolta's *Grease* partnership?

H What does the Spanish word *Caudillo* mean — a title that Franco gave to himself?

AL How many hours pass in the course of James Joyce's *Ulysses*?

SN Which gems are said to represent purity and virginity?

SL Which country has had the most success in the men's Hockey World Cup?

436

G Which eastern country has the world's biggest pig population?

E Who directed *Curse of the Pink Panther* in 1984 and *Victor/Victoria* in 1982?

H Which wall was found, in 1990, to be 600 miles longer than previously thought?

AL What was the name of *She*?

SN How many days does it take the average adult human body to produce 200 billion red blood cells?

SL Which athletic event saw Adrienne Beames as its first sub-three hour female?

(437)

G Which state produces 60% of America's potatoes?

E Who played Jane in the 1981 film version of *Tarzan The Ape Man*?

H Which Roman emperor was baptized on his death bed but is still credited with making Christianity Rome's official religion?

AL Which E.Nesbit novel features three well-trained children called Peter, Roberta and Phyllis

SN What grain has varieties including Purple Straw, Comeback and Federation?

SL Who said: "I can cope with being thrown out of the Labour Party, but I can't cope with Liverpool beating Everton 4-1"?

(438)

G Which northern holiday resort's tallest building houses England's biggest dance hall?

E Which of Dorothy's *Wizard of Oz* companions was called Hickory?

H Which century saw Russia adopt the Gregorian calendar?

AL Which legendary monster was the result of Queen Pasiphae's dalliance with a bull?

SN Which part of your body should be stroked to demonstrate your Babinski Reflex?

SL What colour is motor racing's caution flag?

(439)

G What is the modern name for the city of Angora?

E Who died on the same day as Tommy Trinder after rising to fame as the voice of Bugs Bunny?

H Which Alexander was 'Great'?

AL What did the old woman who lived in a shoe give her children for supper?

SN On what number is the sexagesimal system based?

SL Who, at the end of the 1989-90 season, was Derby County's most capped player?

(440)

G Which country's national anthem is *The Soldier's Song*?

E What kind of lager was advertised by an Old English sheepdog?

H Which company's first ship was the *Britannia*?

AL Which of Shakespeare's 'Henrys' was being performed when the Globe Theatre burnt to the ground?

SN Of what variety of plant is this saguaro the biggest?

SL Which jockey made a come-back in 1990 after rather a taxing lay-off from racing?

G Which US state is home to the famous Knott's Berry Farm?

E Who did Cheryl Ladd once refer to as 'Chuck's Cherubs'?

H Who was the groom when Lord Lichfield gave away Bianca Rosa Perez-Mora?

AL Which famous Cornish novelist died in 1989 at the age of 81?

SN How many noses does an ant have?

SL Which Earl tossed a coin with Sir Charles Bunbury to decide which of their names would be used for a horse race they'd started?

— 442

G Which condiment do the Dutch traditionally serve with chips?

E Which TV show's final episode was a two-and-a-half hour special called *Goodbye, Farewell and Amen*?

H Who played the organ at Bob Geldof and Paula Yates' second wedding to each other?

AL How many sygnets are there in the *Swan Lake* 'Dance of the Cygnets'?

SN What do worker bees feed to their larvae, that is supposed to have heathy-food properties for humans?

SL Which team was followed by Ally's Army in the 1978 World Cup?

443

G How many US states include the word 'New' in their name?

E Who composed the four songs that gave Deacon Blue a 1990 chart-topping E.P.?

H Who made newspaper headlines by marrying his third cousin in 1947?

AL What was the name of *The Barber of Seville*?

SN What colour light is produced by magnesium lamps?

SL Who knocked out Gerry Coetzee and told him: "That's cricket old boy"?

444

G What name is given to a Scottish fishing and hunting guide?

E What did Mavis call the male budgie that flew into her home to replace Harriet?

H What name was given to the computerization of the Stock Exchange?

AL On what are clowns' faces painted, to register their copyright?

SN What is dangling if you've got a limp trapezium?

SL Who was the first person to score a maximum snooker 147 in front of TV cameras, although the cameras weren't switched on at the time!?

G In which Indian state do most of the country's Sikhs eat their curry?

E Which animated TV character's favourite song is *Campdown Races*?

H In which country did Edward marry Mrs Simpson?

AL Which Sunday newspaper brought out a special midweek edition to report on the sale of the *House of Fraser*?

SN What British animal lives in a form?

SL Who owns Ascot racecourse?

Not available — 446

G Which country is refered to as 'Ecosse' by comperes of the Eurovision Song Contest?

E Which 1986 movie told the brief life story of pop idol Ritchie Valens?

H How many years of the 1940s saw clothes rationing in Britain?

AL Whose *Household Management* was originally sold as a part-work?

SN What colour eyes do most Siberian huskies have?

SL Who described his moustache as "A kind of shield. The water slides off it and I can go faster"?

447

G What name was given to the line surveyed in the 1760s as dividing America's free states from slave states?

E How many seats are there in the TV Batmobile?

H With which three islands is Napoleon usually connected?

AL Which book did the Vatican condemn as being blasphemous in March 1989?

SN What colour bones does a garfish have?

SL How many dogs take part in a normal British greyhound race?

G What is the official currency of Puerto Rico?

E Which record company produced the 1978 movie *The Wiz*?

H Who resigned as leader of South Africa's National Party after suffering a stroke in 1989?

AL Under what religion was author Salman Rushdie brought up?

SN What can be anal, dorsal and pectoral?

SL How many strokes compared to par is a 'Double Bogey'?

(449)

G Which Lincolnshire town, no matter what anyone from Plymouth says, was the start of the *Mayflower's* journey to America?

E Which of Dorothy's *Wizard of Oz* companions was called Hunk?

H Who was imprisoned in 1923 for trying to overthrow the Bavarian government?

AL Which Rossini opera is subtitled *The Useless Precaution*?

SN What usually happens to a baby approximately 280 days after its conception?

SL What was jockey Scobie Breasley's first name?

(450)

G Which is the largest country of Scandinavia?

E Which 1989 blockbuster movie found journalists Alex Knox and Vicki Vale tracking down the hero's identity?

H What first for Britain did the London Co-op claim in 1948?

AL What was Louisa Alcott's middle initial?

SN Out of which part of an insect's body do the wings grow?

SL Which Harry is part of this boxer's best-known catchphrase

(451)

G Which English town boasts the tomb of King Edmund who was later canonized?

E Whose first screen words were "Gif me a viskey, ginger ale on the side, and don't be stingy, baby"?

H Which war lasted from 1950 to 1953?

AL Which book tells us that "All animals are equal, but some animals are more equal than others"?

SN What is the typical cruising speed of a housefly: 5,8,10 or 15 kilometres per hour?

SL Which legendary footballer was nicknamed 'The Black Pearl'?

(452)

G Which famous Mexican mountain's name is the ancient Aztec 'Smoking Mountain'?

E Which 1972 US Steve Miller record had the last laugh when it finally reached the UK top ten in 1990?

H Which Richard was murdered at Pontefract Castle in 1400?

AL What fruit was embroidered on the handkerchief that led to Desdemona's death?

SN What shape results from slicing a cone parallel to the sloping edge?

SL Which court game is Malaysia's national sport?

453

G What is the eagle eating, that looks as though it's about to impale itself on a cactus, on the Mexican flag?

E Which single didn't get banned by the BBC despite the line: "Candy never lost her head even when she was giving head"?

H How old was Princess Isabella of France when she married Richard II?

AL How did this famous dancer die?

SN Which semi-precious stone was known as 'The Bishops' Stone' because of its popularity in bishops' rings?

SL What is your average speed if you run a four-minute mile?

454

G What crop is grown on almost ninety per cent of the cultivated land in Mauritius?

E Who is the only British singer to have come second in the Eurovision Song Contest on two occasions?

H What was the first major battle of the Hundred Years' War?

AL Which famous Frenchman died on stage whilst taking part in one of his own plays?

SN Would a pig have been able to swim if it had fallen off the Ark?

SL Which sporting question has the answer 'Pickles the dog'?

455

G Which country is sub-divided into Sabah, Malaya and Sarawak?

E Which blind singer supported the Rolling Stones on their 1972 American tour?

H What was the religion of the Saracens who fought against the Crusaders?

AL What shape is a painting or relief if it is described as 'tondo'?

SN Which American state has an element named after it?

SL Which catering organization sponsors the International Junior Tennis Challenge Series?

456

G What is the former country of Nyasaland now called?

E Which song, written by folksy Ewan McColl, became a huge hit for Roberta Flack after it was played in the film *Play Misty For Me*?

H Which country's throne had 13 claimants when Margaret, the Maid of Norway died?

AL Who sculpted Hyde Park's controversial *Rima*?

SN Which has more bones — a left arm or a right leg?

SL Would East and West Germany have topped the 1988 Olympic medals table if they had competed as one country?

457

G What is the unit of currency in Colombia and Uruguay?

E Which comedian did Mack Sennett discover playing a drunk in a 1912 touring production of *A Night In A London Music Hall*?

H Which US TV announcer was the first to broadcast nationally that John Kennedy had been shot?

AL What term can be applied to any art that doesn't represent a recognizable object?

SN Of which flower family is the apple a member?

SL Which is the longest Olympic event?

458

G Which Latin American country spends 'Balboas' in memory of the first European to view the Pacific Ocean?

E Which popular young film star danced topless in the 1935 Hollywood musical *Curly Top*?

H Who was admitted to Parkland Memorial Hospital, Dallas, as "Patient 24740 — White male"?

AL Which movie superstar came to London in 1989 to fill the role of Shylock?

SN What is a baby cod called?

SL Who was the first Olympic athletics gold medallist to be disqualified after the event?

459

G Who did both Costa Rica and El Salvador commemorate when naming their unit of currency, the 'colon'?

E Which was the first film to gross $70 million?

H Which organization had 40 of its members convicted during a major 1989 Italian trial?

AL Who wrote a book on the subject of his BBC TV show *Around the World in 80 Days*?

SN What are male and female salmon called?

SL Why were the colours selected for the Olympic rings?

460

G Which Canadian city's Royal York Hotel was once the tallest building in the British Empire?

E How many members are there on each *Family Fortunes* team?

H Who said to Mikhail Gorbachev: "You have provided us with an occasion we shall never forget and it is the start of something big"?

AL Which Irish writer and former French Resistance worker died in Paris in 1989?

SN What happens to a sheep's coat if the weather is stormy?

SL Which giant country didn't compete in the Olympics from 1952 to 1984?

461

G Which number is repeated three times if you give the height of Mount Everest in metres?

E Who said: "A man in the house is worth two in the street"?

H In which state did Colonel Sanders set up his first fast-food outlet?

AL Which composer did Stravinsky call "Six foot of Russian gloom"?

SN Which planet was orbited by *Mariner Nine* in 1972?

SL What is the main ingredient in tasteless, but apparently healthy, tofu?

462

G After whom was Venezuela's currency named?

E Which actor, born Ramon Estevez, has played both John and Robert Kennedy?

H Which British political party admitted in 1989 that it had only 11,000 members?

AL What name is given to a sculpted male figure replacing a column to support architecture?

SN What plant was named after Leonard Fuchs the naturalist?

SL Which country hosted the Olympics in 1976 and failed to win a gold medal?

463

G Which is the third-largest country in the world and has almost 25% of the world's population?

E Whose 1989 tour of the UK became known as *The Nude Tour*?

H Were Huguenots, Catholic or Protestant?

AL Whose 'Dong' had 'A luminous nose'?

SN Which is negative — anode or cathode?

SL Which famous cricket ground has the River Effra running underneath it?

464

G Which county is home to louts from Louth?

E Who told the *Carry On* team to "Stop messing about"?

H What is the highest rank in the British peerage after that of Royal Prince?

AL Why was George Smiley's organization called *The Circus*?

SN Which bird of prey is the national symbol of Iceland?

SL Which game is played for the Iroquois Cup?

465

G Which Scottish loch is overlooked by Urquhart Castle?

E What did Harry Enfield's 'Loadsamoney' character do for a living?

H Which actor married millionairess Barbara Hutton in 1942, the couple being dubbed 'Cash and Cary'?

AL Which literary spy was called "The Head Eunuch" by his first boss and "My Darling Teddy-Bear" by his secretary?

SN What is the proper name of the bird of prey known as the 'windhover'?

SL What colour belt is usually supplied with a judo suit?

466

G Which country's name means 'Little Venice'?

E What was Cyril's job in the TV commercial that said: "Nice one Cyril"?

H Which two continents have never seen major military conflict?

AL Which writer's c.v. includes: "Banker, Journalist, Stockbroker and secret work for the Director of Naval Intelligence"?

SN What would be stuck in your teeth if you had just chewed a Norfolk Giant?

SL What are sticking out over the end of the board if a surfer 'Hangs five'?

467

G Which is the only month of the year when Greenland's average temperature is above freezing?

E Which funny female once said: "I always thought Coq au Vin was love in a lorry"?

H Which American clergyman founded the Southern Christian Leadership Conference in 1957?

AL What nationality was Ivor Novello?

SN What type of animal would be doing what, if a dik-dik started spronging?

SL What is your sport if you perform a Tsukahara Tuck?

468

G Which country are you in if you are on a train called the *Silver Fern*?

E Which band's first album had a picture of the Hindenburg airship on its sleeve?

H Which car manufacturer was the first American to be awarded Hitler's Supreme Order of the German Eagle?

AL Which Grecian novel by Nikos Kazantzakis became an Academy Award-winning film in 1964?

SN What is the more common name for this creature's 'vibrissae'?

SL Which famous cocktail is Churchill's mother said to have invented in a New York nightclub?

469

G Which US state was named in honour of Queen Henrietta Maria?

E Which actress could be heard puffing and panting at the end of Rod Stewart's *Tonight's the Night*?

H How many times has the body of Eva Peron lain in state and been buried?

AL What five words precede Shakespeare's line: "And all the men and women merely players"?

SN How many feet does a mollusc such as a common garden snail have?

SL What do you arrange if your hobby is 'Ikebana'?

470

G Which explorer gave his name to the strait separating Tierra del Fuego from the South American mainland?

E Which song from the Beatles' *White Album* was a 1983 hit for Siouxsie and the Banshees?

H Who represented the Queen at John F. Kennedy's funeral?

AL Which 20th century artistic movement took its name at random from a dictionary, coming up with a French word for 'hobbyhorse'?

SN What mammal can jump the highest?

SL What game is played by the Indianapolis Colts and the Denver Broncos?

471

G Which river has Hong Kong at its mouth?

E Which 'page 3 girl' once said: "I've always been a lot more maturer than what I am"?

H Which William was Orange?

AL What is the better known name of Mr. I. N. Davies?

SN Who developed X-rays and was the first winner of a Nobel Prize for Physics?

SL Which country was amongst the top five medal winners in the 1988 Olympics but won't compete in the 1992 or 1996 games?

472

G Who designed the Italian national flag?

E Which pop superstar's wife had a part opposite Nellie Boswell in *Bread*?

H Which year saw Britain join the EEC?

AL Who is said to have been inspired to write *Dracula* after a nightmare, due to eating crabs?

SN Which takes the longer to ferment, mild beers or strong lagers?

SL In which weight did Michael Spinks win his 1976 Olympic gold?

473

G Which African lake is the world's third-largest inland body of water?

E Which American band is alway at the bottom of any alphabetical list of hit record makers?

H What was the nationality of the executioner who was imported to separate Anne Boleyn's head from her shoulders?

AL Which writer did the boxing-loving Marquess of Queensbury accuse of sodomy?

SN What is 'hypotension'?

SL From what occasion did the Greek calendar begin?

474

G Which European country claims the world's oldest national flag design?

E What was the name of the dance named after the *Woodentop's* dog?

H Which former prime minister was called Baillie Vass by *Private Eye*?

AL By what name is John Clayton, the son of Lord Greystoke, better known?

SN Who once said: "I can train a dog in five minutes, training the owner takes longer"?

SL Which Scottish sport is controlled by the WHAA?

475

G Which London park would a man visit if he wanted to walk along the Ladies Mile?

E Which film star's face can be found on his own brands of American sauce and salad dressing?

H Which pioneering delivery service pledged to deliver the goods in 10 days?

AL Which Shakespeare play was the inspiration for a Prokofiev ballet?

SN What can be true, false, or floating?

SL What is the equivalent of America's Boardwalk in a British game of *Monopoly*?

476

G Which colour on the French flag is given the smallest area?

E Which member of sixties band Curved Air went on to become a Police man?

H How old was Horatio Nelson when he first joined the navy to see the world?

AL What are the six characters "in search of", in the title of Luigi Pirandello's best-known play?

SN What was the international radio code for the letter 'A' before it was changed to Alpha?

SL What did the *BSA* company originally manufacture?

477

G Which European country plants grapes on one-fifth of its agricultural land?

E Which Prince film included the hit *When Doves Cry*?

H Who was the first person to fly over the South Pole — Sam Segul, Dickie Byrd or Robin Redbreast?

AL What name is shared by one of Prince Charles' female friends and the older marsupial in the *Winnie-the-Pooh* stories?

SN Which scientist claimed that genius was 1 per cent inspiration and 99 per cent perspiration?

SL With what is a dish cooked *á la Bretonne* garnished?

478

G Which is Pakistan's largest city?

E Which classic hit record was written by Jay Gorney and E.Y. Harburg in the depths of the 1932 depression?

H Who resigned as Ireland's prime minister in 1989?

AL Which country's art is imitated in European works called 'chinoiserie'?

SN What metal is added to petrol to prevent knocking?

SL What term is used by archers for the centre of the target?

479

G Which river is held back by Switzerland's 'Grande Dixence' dam?

E Which band was this infamous character in before he joined the Sex Pistols?

H Which 17th century war began with the raising of the Royal Standard at Nottingham?

AL What two words appeared on the bottle that Alice drank from in *Alice In Wonderland*?

SN What is the colour of a sorrel horse?

SL What does "Dolce Vino" mean to an Italian?

480

G Which country contains most of the Kalahari desert?

E Which 1986 movie found Paul Newman once again cashing in on his Fast Eddie Felson role from *The Hustler*?

H What was formed in 1831 to help control French possessions in Africa?

AL Which fictional sleuth had a maid called Gwen?

SN What have you had checked if your condition is described as either diastolic or systolic?

SL Which brewery's lager features the date 1664 on its can?

481

G Which city would you be in if you hung your Pirelli calendar in the Pirelli skyscraper?

E Which movie hears Groucho Marx saying: "One morning I shot an elephant in my pyjamas. How he got into my pyjamas I'll never know"?

H Which weddng anniversary should the Queen and Prince Philip celebrate in 1997?

AL Which Biblical character is said to have been handed the meteorite that is the focal point of pilgrims to Mecca?

SN Which metal resists corrosion better than all others?

SL Who performs on the uneven parallel bars — male or female gymnasts?

482

G Which strait between two of Norway's Lofoten Islands has given its name to any turbulent confusion?

E Who had just been jilted at the altar on *EastEnders* when 60 prisoners wrecked their Dartmoor cells in 1986?

H What piece of Jack Ruby memorabilia became the subject of a controversial sale attempt in 1990?

AL Which famous artist took up painting with his left hand when he lost the use of his right hand at the age of 60?

SN Where would you go to look for littoral creatures?

SL Who broke the world land speed record in 1927, 1928, 1931, 1932, 1933 and twice in 1935?

483

G Which Normandy town boasts the tomb of William the Conqueror?

E Which superb British band of 'Nutty Boys' split up in 1986?

H What did Gordon Cooper do all by himself that Americans have done with someone else ever since?

AL Which famous children's writer's first names were James Matthew?

SN What type of bird can be a Canvas Back?

SL What nationality was the second man to run a sub-four-minute mile?

484

G Which country's Grand Canal is the world's longest man-made waterway?

E Who owns the Beatles' back catalogue of songs and refused to let the Beastie Boys record *I'm Down*?

H What did fellow countrymen call this man?

AL Who wrote the words of the Women's Institute anthem *Jerusalem*?

SN What kind of fruit can be a Yellow Egg?

SL How many times was Muhammad Ali punched when he lost his world title in 1967?

93

485

G This European capital city is the setting for a popular fictonal detective tv series. What is its name and what is the detective's name?

E Which musical was directed onto film in 1985 by Richard Attenborough?

H How many of the USA's presidents were not born in North America?

AL How do Americans spell pyjamas?

SN On what fruit tree would you expect to find mistletoe?

SL Which field event saw Chionis register a record distance of 23 feet 1.5 inches, at the Olympics in 656 BC?

486

G Which country is home to the Dayaks?

E What kind of parties did the police vow to stamp out in a 1989 press statement?

H How long, to the nearest hour, did it take Alcock and Brown to fly across the Atlantic?

AL Which day's child is blithe, bonny, good and gay?

SN Which television programme's theme music was played at the commissioning ceremony for the first Space Shuttle?

SL Which team won the 1988-89 Football League Championship with a 2-0 win in their final match against Liverpool?

487

G Which South American country has a flag that is different on each side?

E Which pop superstar had a bit-part as a chauffeur on *Bread*?

H Which 1990 film found the police warning that children shouldn't go into sewers?

AL What does 'Brer' mean in the 'Brer Rabbit' stories?

SN Which bits of their bodies would be touching if he held her Girdle of Venus in his Mount of Jupiter?

SL How many medals did Russian gymnast Aleksandr Ditiatin win in the 1980 Olympic games, to set a new record?

488

G Which is the largest city on the island of Cyprus?

E Which John Lennon hit did Roxy Music record as a tribute?

H Who surrendered aboard the *Bellerophon* on 15th July 1815?

AL Who does Pierre Bexukhov decide to assassinate in *War and Peace*?

SN As what is the regularly occurring female complaint dysmenorrhoea usually described, on an aspirin packet?

SL What piece of sporting equipment killed George II's son, the Prince of Wales?

489

G What objects are the kangaroos carrying on the Western Australia coat of arms?

E Who leads, and is also married to, one of the Coconuts?

H Which war saw the bazooka make its debut?

AL For which of Dante's works did Botticelli provide hellishly brilliant illustrations?

SN Where should you rub the ointment if you have Herpes Labialis?

SL Which racing driver was known as the 'Clockwork Mouse'?

490

G Which Scandinavian capital is built on nine bridge-connected islands?

E What did Bob Geldof have sticking out of his top pocket when he received his knighthood from the Queen?

H Which 'quality' Sunday newspaper became a tabloid when Robert Maxwell became a major shareholder in 1990?

AL What kind of clock was invented by swinging scientist Christian Huygens?

SN What has a pinniped got instead of legs?

SL Which football team plays its home matches at Upton Park?

491

G What is the Belgian Congo now called?

E Which member of the *Monty Python* team died during the 10th anniversary celebrations of the show's success?

H What carried Scott's gear on his ill-fated expedition to the South Pole?

AL On which film star was Maggie modelled in Arthur Miller's *After The Fall*?

SN Who founded the German company that merged with *Daimler-Motoren-Gesellschaft* in 1926?

SL What financial breakthrough was made by goalkeeper Nigel Martyn when he was transferred from Bristol Rovers to Crystal Palace in 1989?

492

G Of what is *Stolichnaya* Russia's biggest-selling brand?

E To what was West Virginia changed in Toots and the Maytals reggae version of *Country Roads*?

H Which newsreader separated from her husband Christopher Dare after 22 years of marriage?

AL What kind of bulb did Mohammed recommend as an antidote for snake and scorpion bites?

SN How many points does a starfish have?

SL Which London football team is known as the Lions?

493

G What was the former name of Belize?

E Which star of *The Scapegoat* died at the age of 81 in 1989?

H Which queen was Britain's last Stuart monarch?

AL Which Shakespeare play features a clown called 'Touchstone'?

SN What test did Alfred Binet devise in an effort to identify 'backward' children?

SL What was the largest word on Liverpool's shirts when they played in the 1989 FA Cup Final?

494

G As what are Dubai, Abu Dhabi, Ajman, Sharjah, Ras al Khaimah, Fujairah and Umm al-Qaiwain collectively known?

E Which member of the Blues Brothers died of an accidental drug overdose in 1982?

H Who dissolved Parliament in 1629 and ruled personally until 1640?

AL Which pantomine features a prince with a male companion called 'Dandine'?

SN With which metal was dentist Robert Arthur the first to fill a cavity, in 1855?

SL What is the lowest score that can 'bust' you in a game of Pontoon?

495

G Which city in Pakistan boasts the Badshahi Mosque, the largest in the world?

E Which Mike Oldfield album spent fifteen months in the UK charts before reaching number one?

H Which century saw the War of the Roses?

AL What popular use was found for the Covent Garden Opera House during the years of the Second World War?

SN Which animal's prodigious reproductive habits are the basis for the Fibonacci sequence, which starts: 1,1,2,3,5,8,13...?

SL What is a Spaniard adding to his paella if the label on the carton reads 'azafran'?

496

G What is the principal language of Papua New Guinea?

E Which British singer-songwriter was official top of the bill when John Lennon made his final stage appearance?

H To which country did Mary Queen of Scots return in 1561?

AL Who was the head boy at Greyfriar's School?

SN What is added to soap to make it transparent?

SL Which Grand Slam golf tournament wasn't held between 1940 and 1945?

497

G Which tiny republic is in the hills behind the seaside resort of Rimini?

E Which Andy Fairweather-Low hit did Terry Wogan admit he once almost played, after interviewing Douglas Bader?

H Which country was united by the marriage of Ferdinand of Aragon to Isabella of Castile?

AL What nationality did El Greco adopt?

SN Is your latissimus dorsi above or below your waist?

SL What should a boxer head for when he knocks down his opponent?

498

G What is the capital of the former slave country of Sierra Leone?

E What instrument did Rafael Ravenscroft play with stunning effect on Gerry Rafferty's *Baker Street*?

H Who discovered Nicaragua?

AL Whose Trojan jewels did archaeologist Heinrich Schliemann think he had found, in which he famously decked his wife?

SN Which fruit combines with an orange to make a clementine?

SL What fortified Sicilian wine is traditionally added to zabaglione?

499

G Which country boasts the Gota, the world's longest canal?

E Which creature in *Bambi* was inappropriately called Flower?

H Who met Francois I of France on the Field of the Cloth of Gold?

AL Which city is now the home of Constantinople's famous quartet of equestrian bronzes?

SN Which part of a deer's anatomy were Weimaraner dogs trained to attack?

SL Which chess piece can regularly move in a way that the queen can't imitate?

500

G On which Great Lake would a reflection of the C.N. Tower be seen?

E Of which Police hit did Sting perform a solo version at the Wembley Live Aid concert?

H Which conquest is commemorated by Battle Abbey in Sussex?

AL Of which artistic movement was Aubrey Beardsley a popular exponent?

SN What metal is mixed with aluminium to produce the strong alloy duralumin?

SL What was Robert Culp's sport in the TV series *I Spy*?

501

G In what type of building would you be if you were in Paris' 'Galeries Lafayette'?

E How many Village People gaily sang their way through the *YMCA*?

H What was the capital of England in the Middle Ages?

AL Of which discipline of art were Andy Warhol and Roy Lichtenstein popular exponents?

SN Which two metals mix to produce solder?

SL Which tiny country saw skier Hanni Wenzel win its first ever Olympic gold in 1984?

502

G Which is the biggest city in Italy's Latium province?

E Which river gave its name to the character who took over from Blake as the leader of *Blake's Seven*?

H What was the capital of the USA, prior to Washington DC?

AL Which famous artist was abandoned at birth because the midwife thought he was stillborn?

SN What flows into your house at a rate of 50 cycles per second?

SL What does paper do if stone breaks scissors?

503

G Which country would you visit to eat a Chicken Kiev, in the Cafe Kiev, in Kiev?

E Who was the singing father of the actress who first shot J.R.?

H What was the government position of Lord Thomson who died in the *R101* Airship disaster?

AL Who sold only one painting, *The Red Vineyard*?

SN How many cells do bacteria have?

SL From which city do the American footballing *Dolphins* come?

504

G Which country is home to the second-highest number of native English speakers?

E Which rock band met the Phantom in a 1978 movie?

H Which high English post was held by Frederick Temple and then by his son William?

AL Who drew a freehand circle for the Pope to prove his skill?

SN What kind of acids are bonded together in chains called 'peptides'?

SL Which showjumping event sees the wall getting higher and higher?

(505)

G What is the English name for the Greek island of Kerkira?

E What did Dorothy have to steal from the Wicked Witch of the West?

H Who was the first Pope to choose a double name?

AL Which popular 15th-16th century artist was jailed over homosexuality charges?

SN What does the word anhydrous tell you there is an absence of?

SL Which American president claimed that he would have been a sports writer if he'd had his life to live again?

(506)

G What animal appears on an Australian 50-cent coin?

E Which character on *M*A*S*H* wore a 36B 'Miss Highrise' bra?

H Which politician described the Lonrho Affair as: "The unpleasant and unacceptable face of Capitalism"?

AL Which American artist became famous for his *Saturday Evening Post* cover designs?

SN What name is given to the proteins produced by the body, which react with antigens to make them harmless?

SL Which Yorkshire boxer went five rounds with Muhammad Ali?

(507)

G Which city is the administrative centre of Devon?

E Which was the BBC series about the Majestics, a group of Glaswegian fifties rockers?

H Who is the only British prime minister to have been assassinated?

AL How long, to the nearest year, did it take Michelangelo to paint the Sistine Chapel ceiling?

SN What does the abbreviation DC mean to an electrician?

SL Which West German race track is by far the longest regularly used for Formula I Grand Prix races?

(508)

G Who are the only people in Madras legally allowed to drink alcohol?

E She was known as "the worlds sweetheart" but what was her name and who was her equally famous husband?

H Which American president died during the final minutes of the 18th century?

AL Which famous British artist had himself tied to a ship's mast so that he could paint during a storm?

SN What name is given to two or more electric cells connected together in series?

SL Would I.Q. be accepted as a word in a game of *Scrabble*?

509

G Which island country's coastline is second in length only to that of Canada?

E Which singer mimed to a track from *Dick Tracy* during her 1990 Wembley Stadium concerts?

H Which historical leader is said to have been shot dead by his lover, whilst in the process of poisoning himself?

AL For which George did John Nash build the Brighton Pavilion?

SN What name is given to the green alkaline fluid produced in the liver?

SL Who is cricket's biggest scoring batswoman?

510

G Which West African country's name means 'Lion Mountain' in Portuguese?

E What six words precede "from loneliness to a wedding ring"?

H What did Nell Gwyn catch from Charles II that eventually killed her?

AL Which building in London is Charles Barry and Augustus Pugin's most famous joint venture?

SN What curently in-vogue word describes substances that can be broken down by biological action?

SL Which knighted jockey won his first Derby at the age of 49?

511

G Which country had the world's highest arson rate in 1989?

E Which husband and wife acting duo starred in *The Big Sleep* and *Dark Passage*?

H Which of Henry VIII's wives was his former sister-in-law?

AL Which London street features John Nash's most famous crescent?

SN What are the third group of blood cells along with red and white cells?

SL What medal did Swedish shooting champion Oscar Swahn win in the 1920 Olympics after winning a gold in 1912 at the age of 64?

512

G What word found at the beginning of many Welsh town names, means 'at the mouth of' a river?

E Which year saw Bros and Kylie amongst the stars who recorded *Do they know its Christmas* for Ethiopia?

H Is Yasir Arafat's PLO recognised by the United Nations?

AL Who stabbed Caesar first in Shakespeare's *Julius Caesar*?

SN Of what are bontebok and bongo varieties?

SL Who scored 24 goals for Tottenham Hotspur in the 1989-90 season?

513

G Which country's flag is red with five yellow stars in the corner?

E Which Dennis Weaver TV series was a spin-off from Clint Eastwood's *Coogan's Bluff*?

H Which member of the Royal Family's first names are Marie-Christine?

AL What form of decoration can be Plique-a-jour, Basse-taille and Cloisonne?

SN What four-letter word means the same thing as calcium oxide?

SL Which Olympic distance event rules insist that competitors must maintain unbroken contact with the ground?

514

G Which Canadian province might see geese landing at Gander Airport?

E Which Charlie Chaplin film featured a character called Adenoid Hynkel based on Adolf Hitler?

H Which two European countries joined in the American War of Independence against Britain?

AL Which opera house's name means 'The Staircase'?

SN What is the international radio code word for the letter R?

SL How many barrels does a *Winchester 21* shotgun have?

515

G Which country has problems with its Contra rebels?

E Which film sees a character called Don Lockwood getting exceedingly wet?

H In which city was the treaty signed, to end the American War of Independence?

AL Why couldn't a seventeenth century piano appear with a modern orchestra?

SN Which city gave its name to currents?

SL Which Olympic sport finds competitors using equipment made by Anschutz and Remington?

516

G Which country's secret police were the Tontons Macoutes?

E Whose first film was actually *Plane Crazy* even if everyone does think it was *Steamboat Willie*?

H Which island did Britain capture from the Dutch, in the same year that Napoleon conquered most of Italy?

AL Which planet was 'Mystic' according to Gustav Holst?

SN Where are a bird's barbs?

SL What do Americans call what the British call King prawns?

G Which Scottish city is situated at the mouths of the Dee and the Don?

E In which city does Superman live?

H What was added to Great Britain to form the United Kingdom?

AL What was the land of heroes called in Arthurian legend?

SN What disorder was psychologist O.H.Mowrer's "bed and blanket" method devised to cure?

SL Which former Olympic competitor made news by being banned from driving, after a speeding offence in October 1990?

G Which country attracts tourists to its Reichenbach Falls where Sherlock Holmes supposedly fell to his death?

E What was the surname of Dorothy, the girl who got blown away in *The Wizard of Oz*?

H Who was the first Governor General of India?

AL What is Latin for "and the rest"?

SN Which bird has the biggest eyes?

SL Which cricket ground did Australian Sir Donald Bradman rate as the best in the world?

G Which city's financial whiz-kids are called 'Gnomes'?

E Who was responsible for the voices of Bugs Bunny, Silvester and Tweetie Pie?

H Which city saw 146 British prisoners held in a tiny room in 1756?

AL How many whacks with the axe did Lizzie Borden inflict upon her father according to the rhyme?

SN What is an infant seal called?

SL How many circuits of an Olympic velodrome must a cyclist cover to complete 1000 metres?

G Which European route was dubbed 'The Queen of Roads' when it was completed in 312 BC?

E Which American hero has been played on film by Errol Flynn, Robert Shaw and Ronald Reagan?

H This Royal was known as "The Young Pretender". What was his more common nickname?

AL Who were the subjects of both Peter Brown's *The Love You Make* and Philip Norman's *Shout*?

SN What kind of animal is a pipistrelle

SL How many metres do Olympic highboard divers fall before they get wet?

521

G Which town in Gwent was mentioned in a Marty Wilde hit record title?

E What was the real name of this famous film star?

H Which century saw the abolition of the slave trade in the British Empire?

AL Which Poet Laureate was married to writer Sylvia Plath?

SN What did Archimedes say he would require to move the world, if he had a place to stand?

SL What is the only thing that originally accompanied Yorkshire Pudding?

522

G Which town in Dyfed has a name which is Welsh for "Mouth of the Ystwyth"?

E What is the theatrical equivalent of an Oscar?

H Was there a king of Spain called Joe Bonaparte?

AL Who's Second Symphony is called *The Little Russian*?

SN What is a quarter of a quarter?

SL How many bars would you have to saw through to escape from jail in a game of Monopoly?

523

G What comes down the Labrador Current that are a major threat to shipping?

E Which film finds Jim placing a newspaper ad. in an attempt to find his girlfriend Susan?

H Who was the Queen's first grandchild?

AL Who is the ancient God of woods and shepherds after whom an instrument is named?

SN Which is ammonia solution, an acid or an alkali?

SL Which famous horse race is featured in the film *National Velvet*?

524

G What is the largest city on the Firth of Forth?

E Which $41-million sci-fi movie was directed by David Lynch, and produced by Dino de Laurentiis' daughter, Raffaella?

H Who was assassinated the day before *Dr Who* first appeared on televison?

AL Who wrote the best-selling guitar tutor of all time, *Play In A Day*?

SN Who discovered the breakdown of the colours in the spectrum?

SL Which cricketer was known as 'The Champion'?

525

G What nationality are you if you are a citizen of Condom?

E Which musical instrument is named after the Hawaiian word for 'flea'?

H What style of haircut was banned by the Indonesian government in 1964?

AL Which pop group took their name from the detectives in *Tintin*?

SN How many miles per second must a rocket travel to clear the Earth's gravitational pull?

SL Which sport finds Americans bunting?

526

G Who was Guam's head of state the day after J.F. Kennedy was assassinated?

E As what did Cream dress up to warrant the promotional film for their hit, *I Feel Free*, being banned in America?

H What is the nickname of the 8th Army, famous for their service in World War II, and again in Iraq in 1990?

AL What job did Henri Rousseau have to earn the nickname 'Douanier'?

SN What nationality was this woman, and for what science did she win her second Nobel Prize?

SL In which American sport can you shag flies?

527

G What is the capital of Guatemala?

E Which Irish ballad singer knocked the Beatles' *Sergeant Pepper* album from the number 1 slot on the UK chart?

H Which Queen earned the name 'Gloriana'?

AL Which Plymouth housewife became famous with her delicious paintings of big fat ladies?

SN Which roses have been scientifically proved to last longer — those cut in the morning or those cut in the afternoon?

SL Which is heavier — a volleyball or a soccer ball?

528

G What did Fifi do to bring Honduras into the world headlines in 1974?

E Who was the father of the baby that Marianne Faithfull miscarried in 1968?

H What was unusual about the 1212 Crusade, that is said to have given birth to the story of the Pied Piper?

AL Which Shakespeare play features Arden Forest?

SN How many brains does a silkworm have?

SL Which communist country had the second-highest medal tally at the 1984 Los Angeles Olympics?

529

G What is Guyana's main export?

E What are the names of the husbands of this famous duo?

H Which US President was assassinated in 1901?

AL Who wrote about *The Water Babies*?

SN What do people have an uncontrollable need to do if they suffer from narcolepsy?

SL What did the poetically named Spiridon Belokas do to get himself disqualified from the 1896 Olympic marathon?

530

G Which European country was said to be the same size as the area of Brazilian rainforest burnt by cattle-ranchers in 1988?

E Which movie saw Gene Wilder and Richard Pryor befriending a gross mass murderer called Grossberger?

H Why were pubs in the news on 22nd August 1988?

AL Which city's most famous orchestra is the Halle?

SN What word describes a plant or animal that has been produced by parents who are genetically unlike each other?

SL Which Olympic event's categories include first heavyweight, second heavyweight and super heavyweight?

531

G Which country swore in Ranasinghe Premadasa as its president in 1989?

E Who made her 20th Century Fox debut in *The Virgin Queen* but had no virgin reputation when she starred in *Dynasty*?

H Which London airport saw its first jet land in July 1988?

AL On which Shakespeare play was the film *Forbidden Planet* based?

SN What effect, linked to the increasing quantities of carbon dioxide in the atmosphere, has been blamed for unusual weather conditions?

SL Which has been thrown furthest, the hammer, the women's discus or the women's javelin?

532

G What is the modern English name for the language of Hungary?

E Who had the best selling rock video with *Who's Better Who's Best*?

H Which country was at war with England from 1109 to 1113?

AL Which London church has a famous version of Holman Hunt's *The Light of the World*?

SN How many teats does a female goat have?

SL How did Jeana Yeager and Dick Rutan fly their way into the record books in 1986?

533

G On which island is the Indonesian capital of Djakarta situated?

E Which Elvis Presley song was a major hit for the Fine Young Cannibals?

H Which country was controlled by the Toltecs?

AL Which major London church was designed by J.F. Bentley?

SN Why did early sailors take a lodestone to sea?

SL What surname was common to the gold medal winners in the 1988 Olympic boxing Super Heavyweight and 100 metres sprint?

534

G Which country boasts the site of the Hanging Gardens of Babylon, and the site of the hanging of an *Observer* journalist?

E Which Beatle was arrested on drugs charges on the same day that Paul McCartney married Linda?

H Who was appointed Archbishop of Canterbury in 1162?

AL What was James Abbott McNeill Whistler accused of throwing in the public's face?

SN What does the anemometer at an airport measure?

SL What was the most common name for gold medal winners at the 1988 Summer Olympics?

535

G Which country supplies 80 per cent of the world's dates, and will always include 1990 as a date in its history books?

E Which single did David Bowie release to coincide with the first manned lunar landing?

H What Japanese title was passed down through the Minamoto, Ashikaga and Tokugawa families, from the 1300s to 1868?

AL Which bit of the actress's body formed the sofa, in the room that Man Ray based on Mae West?

SN Which row of a typewriter keyboard has the most vowels?

SL Which boxer appeared at the Old Bailey, charged with shooting Frank Warren?

536

G Which range of Jamaican mountains give their name to a famous coffee?

E Which Rolling Stones' hit entered the UK charts on the day of Brian Jones' funeral?

H What is the better-known title of Tamujin, 'Emperor within the Seas'?

AL Which Italian painter gave his name to a cocktail?

SN Why was the mongoose introduced to Martinique?

SL Which country won the 1988 Summer Olympic men's hockey gold medal?

537

G Which island's natives called their home Te-Pito-O-Te-Henua which means 'The Navel of the World'?

E What did Paul McCartney wear on his feet on the *Abbey Road* album sleeve?

H How many years old was Henry III when he became King of England?

AL What was the Duke of Wellington's famous four-word reply, when Harriette Wilson threatened to expose him, in her autobiography?

SN What occurs in one out of every 490,000 human births?

SL Which country won the 1988 Olympic coxless pairs rowing gold medal?

538

G What does a Japanese businessman abroad mean when he looks towards home in the early morning and says: "Nihon Koku"?

E Which female blues singer bled to death in 1934 after being refused entry to a whites-only hospital?

H Which century saw the Chinese make the first use of rockets in a war?

AL Where did Chaucer's pilgrims meet prior to their journey to Canterbury?

SN What is the date if the day before yesterday was 12th Night?

SL Which northern English football club was originally known as Newton Heath?

539

G Which London market was moved to Nine Elms?

E Did Margaret Thatcher attend the Wembley, Nelson Mandela extravaganza for a short while?

H What did Seneca do in AD60 because Nero told him to do it?

AL What was H.G. Wells' first novel?

SN What canine-sounding name is given to sounds with a frequency of under 20 cycles per second?

SL Who partnered Pam Shriver in her 1982 Wimbledon ladies' doubles win?

540

G What is Abyssinia now called?

E Which Prefab Sprout hit had the chorus "Hot dog, jumping frog, Albuquerque"?

H Whose illegitimate grandson was Gary Gilmore, the man who failed to escape death by firing squad in 1977?

AL Which poet inherited the title Baron of Rochdale?

SN From which wood were water pipes originally made?

SL Who partnered Tracy Austin in her 1980 Wimbledon mixed doubles win?

541

G Which is the longest river in Scotland?

E Who joined Chubby Checker on his 1988 return rehash of *The Twist*?

H What went up in 1961 and didn't come down until 1990?

AL Who is the President in *All The President's Men*?

SN How many laws of motion did Sir Isaac Newton come up with?

SL Who was the first woman to achieve sporting wins worth $100,000 in a year?

542

G How many hours would you have to put your watch forward on a winter trip from London to Moscow?

E How is Pepa spelt in the name of the spicy female pop duo Salt and Pepa?

H Which former drink-drive campaigner resigned as a minister after an alleged drink-drive incident in Bournemouth?

AL Which patriotic piece of Americana was written by Francis Scott Key?

SN What seven-letter word means mean?

SL Which country boasts Ajax as one of its top football clubs?

543

G What is the name of this canal and which two seas does it link?

E Which band sang *Tango In The Night*?

H What was found in Abraham Lincoln's coffin when it was opened in 1901?

AL Who invented the five towns of Bursley, Hanbridge, Knype, Longshaw and Turnhill?

SN What are there sixteen of, in one ounce?

SL Which major tennis tournament was first contested in 1900?

544

G Which castle saw the investiture of Prince Charles?

E Which Beatles single title was adapted for a Voice of the Beehive hit album title?

H Which English king had 18 legitimate children?

AL What description for Johnson was first used by Smollett in a letter to John Wilkes?

SN Which plastic was invented way back in 1865?

SL Who fell off 'Good Prospect' and has hit the headlines by falling off horses ever since?

545

G Which Southeast Asian country is irrigated by the Irrawaddy?

E Which reggae singer is backed by the Melody Makers?

H Which Princess was given a name meaning 'Bringer of Joy' in 1988?

AL Before which century must a book be printed to qualify as an 'Incunabula'?

SN What does someone attending a wedding probably have in their pockets if they smell of naphthalene?

SL Which James Bond film saw tennis star Vijay Amritraj playing a cameo role?

546

G Which theme park has the greater acreage of land to go on spreading over — *Disneyworld* or *Disneyland*?

E Which one-name female sang lead vocals on Coldcut's *Doctorin' The House* before having huge solo success?

H Which summer would have seen the end of the world if the Jehovah's Witnesses had got their facts right?

AL This man designed which famous rock group's lips-and-lolling-tongue logo?

SN What other metal joins iron and nickel to form stainless steel?

SL Which film role was filled by 1936 Olympic Decathlon winner Glenn Morris?

547

G Which country's Uttar Pradesh state is almost the same size as France?

E Which British pop band celebrated their 25th anniversary in 1988 with a number 1 single?

H What name was shared by the first British paddle steamer and the world's first jet airliner?

AL What name is given to individual frames from animated movies?

SN What type of creature are you eating if you are served abalone?

SL Which sport is played between Oxford and Cambridge for the Bowring Bowl?

548

G Which common British first name is France's most common surname?

E Which Supremes hit also charted for Bananarama?

H With what were sailors issued for the first time in 1857?

AL What was the name of Dr. Doolittle's double ended llama?

SN What change takes place in the colour of goldfish if they are kept in the dark for long enough?

SL How many official English greyhound races are run over distances of a mile or more?

549

G Which city's main tourist attraction is the Manneken Pis?

E What two words appeared in brackets after Enya's number 1 hit title *Orinoco Flow* ?

H For whom was the Palace of Versailles built?

AL Which family was by far the most famous literary creation of J.R. Wyss?

SN Why is Ben Johnson definitely not a pharmacophobic?

SL For which World Cup cricket team did Lancashire's Wasim Akram play?

550

G Which bird did Bugsy Siegel name the first hotel on Las Vegas' 'strip' after?

E Which pop singer is the subject of a museum close to the entrance of Florida's *Disneyworld*?

H Which Dorset castle saw the murder of Edward the Martyr?

AL Who remained happy by name, even after losing all of his money in the *South Sea Bubble*?

SN How do gardeners remember Michael Begon?

SL How has a golf ball gone into the hole if it has gone 'via the tradesman's entrance'?

551

G Which is the most northerly of the Channel Islands?

E What did Starturn on 45 Pints 'Pump Up' in their 1988 hit title?

H Which king allowed himself to be publicly flogged as penance for the death of Thomas a Becket?

AL Which Kenneth Graham character knew twice as much as "the clever men at Oxford"?

SN Which long-tailed American mammal washes its food before eating it?

SL How many days are devoted to the ten events of the Olympic decathlon?

552

G What does a 'gabbawallah' bring you at around midday in India?

E What five words precede "I've hungered for your touch" in the song *Unchained Melody*?

H Which country's voters have been offered the choice of the ZANU and ZAPU parties?

AL Does the *Mona Lisa* wear a single strand of pearls around her neck?

SN By what do people feel their skin is being stimulated, when formication takes place?

SL What is the main ingredient in felafel?

553

G Which large country's first female Governor-General was Jeanne Sauve?

E Which pop siblings asked *When Will I Be Famous* and then became very famous?

H Whose debating technique was described as "Like being savaged by a dead sheep"?

AL Who preceded John Fletcher as the principal writer to the King's Men?

SN Which American adviser to Margaret Thatcher won the 1976 Nobel Prize for Economics?

SL What nationality were all but four of the runners in the first modern Olympic marathon?

554

G Which West Country city is served by Lulsgate Airport?

E Which band regally shot up the charts with *Magic Years-The Complete Set*?

H What colour is the number 10 on the door of Number 10?

AL Who captained the *Pequod*?

SN Which animal joins the Cape buffalo, elephant, lion and leopard as one of Africa's 'Big Five'?

SL What is the highest possible bid in Contract Bridge?

555

G In which mountain range would you find Andorra?

E Whose rock'n'rolling *Anniversary Waltz* was a 1990 mega-hit?

H In which country were Roman emperors Trajan and Hadrian born?

AL Which opera is subtitled *The Slave of Duty*?

SN Which North American creature is the world's largest land carnivore?

SL Which football manager was knighted in 1968?

556

G Which Asian country's exotic nightlife used to centre on Bugis Street?

E Which Hans Christian Andersen story was Disney's 1990 animated offering?

H Who was 'Thazza' in Private Eye if Paul Gascoigne was 'Gazza'?

AL Which part of the body's anatomy has been dissected in Rembrandt's famous painting of an anatomy lesson?

SN What cloth is produced from tangled moistened fibres of hair and wool, heated and rolled together?

SL Which part of Germany, East or West, appeared as GDR on the Olympic scoreboard?

557

G With the manufacture of what item of clothing is the French town of Grenoble particularly associated?

E Which 1988 television fund-raising event attracted more British viewers than Live Aid?

H How old was Henry VIII when he became king?

AL Whose 10th symphony was unfinished?

SN From which of the sun's rays does what's left of the ozone layer protect us?

SL At what other sport did this cricketer captain England?

558

G What two astronomical objects appear on the Turkish flag?

E Which oddly named band went 'From Langley Park to Memphis'?

H What nationality would the original Neanderthal Man have been?

AL As what is Beethoven's 3rd symphony better known?

SN Which Dorset holiday resort is famous for Mary Anning's fossil finds?

SL How old was Floyd Patterson when he won the 1952 Olympic middleweight gold medal?

559

G Which country produces real Parmesan to grate on top of your pasta?

E Which pop singer was *Bare* in a 1990 book title?

H Which British king reigned for just 325 days?

AL Which opera singer, known as 'La Stupenda', retired in 1990?

SN What substance is the dust that forms, when a laser cuts a diamond?

SL What name is given to five of a kind in a game of Yahtzee?

560

G Which city is the kick-off point for most attempts on Mount Everest?

E Which band's sixth member, Ian Stewart, was rarely seen on stage and died in 1985?

H Which English queen ruled for 45 years?

AL What colour stockings were worn by Shakespeare's Malvolio?

SN Which part of the body consumes 40 per cent of the blood's oxygen?

SL Who won his first Derby in 1954 on Never Say Die?

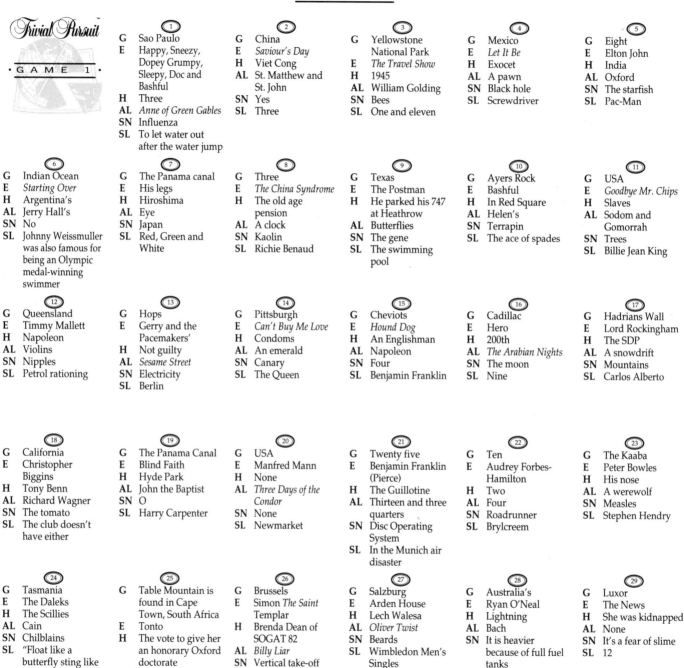

Trivial Pursuit™ · GAME 1 ·

1
- G Sao Paulo
- E Happy, Sneezy, Dopey Grumpy, Sleepy, Doc and Bashful
- H Three
- AL *Anne of Green Gables*
- SN Influenza
- SL To let water out after the water jump

2
- G China
- E *Saviour's Day*
- H Viet Cong
- AL St. Matthew and St. John
- SN Yes
- SL Three

3
- G Yellowstone National Park
- E *The Travel Show*
- H 1945
- AL William Golding
- SN Bees
- SL One and eleven

4
- G Mexico
- E *Let It Be*
- H Exocet
- AL A pawn
- SN Black hole
- SL Screwdriver

5
- G Eight
- E Elton John
- H India
- AL Oxford
- SN The starfish
- SL Pac-Man

6
- G Indian Ocean
- E *Starting Over*
- H Argentina's
- AL Jerry Hall's
- SN No
- SL Johnny Weissmuller was also famous for being an Olympic medal-winning swimmer

7
- G The Panama canal
- E His legs
- H Hiroshima
- AL Eye
- SN Japan
- SL Red, Green and White

8
- G Three
- E *The China Syndrome*
- H The old age pension
- AL A clock
- SN Kaolin
- SL Richie Benaud

9
- G Texas
- E The Postman
- H He parked his 747 at Heathrow
- AL Butterflies
- SN The gene
- SL The swimming pool

10
- G Ayers Rock
- E Bashful
- H In Red Square
- AL Helen's
- SN Terrapin
- SL The ace of spades

11
- G USA
- E *Goodbye Mr. Chips*
- H Slaves
- AL Sodom and Gomorrah
- SN Trees
- SL Billie Jean King

12
- G Queensland
- E Timmy Mallett
- H Napoleon
- AL Violins
- SN Nipples
- SL Petrol rationing

13
- G Hops
- E Gerry and the Pacemakers'
- H Not guilty
- AL *Sesame Street*
- SN Electricity
- SL Berlin

14
- G Pittsburgh
- E *Can't Buy Me Love*
- H Condoms
- AL An emerald
- SN Canary
- SL The Queen

15
- G Cheviots
- E *Hound Dog*
- H An Englishman
- AL Napoleon
- SN Four
- SL Benjamin Franklin

16
- G Cadillac
- E Hero
- H 200th
- AL *The Arabian Nights*
- SN The moon
- SL Nine

17
- G Hadrians Wall
- E Lord Rockingham
- H The SDP
- AL A snowdrift
- SN Mountains
- SL Carlos Alberto

18
- G California
- E Christopher Biggins
- H Tony Benn
- AL Richard Wagner
- SN The tomato
- SL The club doesn't have either

19
- G The Panama Canal
- E Blind Faith
- H Hyde Park
- AL John the Baptist
- SN O
- SL Harry Carpenter

20
- G USA
- E Manfred Mann
- H None
- AL *Three Days of the Condor*
- SN None
- SL Newmarket

21
- G Twenty five
- E Benjamin Franklin (Pierce)
- H The Guillotine
- AL Thirteen and three quarters
- SN Disc Operating System
- SL In the Munich air disaster

22
- G Ten
- E Audrey Forbes-Hamilton
- H Two
- AL Four
- SN Roadrunner
- SL Brylcreem

23
- G The Kaaba
- E Peter Bowles
- H His nose
- AL A werewolf
- SN Measles
- SL Stephen Hendry

24
- G Tasmania
- E The Daleks
- H The Scillies
- AL Cain
- SN Chilblains
- SL "Float like a butterfly sting like a bee"

25
- G Table Mountain is found in Cape Town, South Africa
- E Tonto
- H The vote to give her an honorary Oxford doctorate
- AL None
- SN The lark
- SL Italy

26
- G Brussels
- E Simon *The Saint* Templar
- H Brenda Dean of SOGAT 82
- AL *Billy Liar*
- SN Vertical take-off and landing
- SL Crystallite

27
- G Salzburg
- E Arden House
- H Lech Walesa
- AL *Oliver Twist*
- SN Beards
- SL Wimbledon Men's Singles

28
- G Australia's
- E Ryan O'Neal
- H Lightning
- AL Bach
- SN It is heavier because of full fuel tanks
- SL *The Guardian*

29
- G Luxor
- E The News
- H She was kidnapped
- AL None
- SN It's a fear of slime
- SL 12

30
G The Niagara River
E George Dixon
H He got on his bike and looked for work
AL He shot himself
SN *Flyer*
SL Daley Thompson

31
G The Canaries
E Bela Lugosi
H The Tolpuddle Martyrs
AL Salman Rushdie
SN Radioactivity
SL Chas and Dave

32
G Spain
E Nemesis
H The *Marchioness*
AL Portugal's
SN Six
SL Ayr

33
G The USA's
E Steve Nallon
H *P & O Ferries*
AL Cleo Laine
SN 90
SL The Jockey Club

34
G Israel
E Mia Farrow
H San Francisco
AL Elizabeth Schwarzkopf's
SN Women
SL India Pale Ale

35
G Pink
E 1988
H Harrods
AL Madame Butterfly
SN Seven
SL The Friendship Games

36
G San Francisco's
E Ronald Reagan
H Aldo Moro's
AL *Intermezzo*
SN Bacterium
SL England

37
G France
E Michael Jackson
H 1978
AL Dr. Benjamin Spock
SN His tongue
SL Coventry City

38
G Lesbosians
E Kelly Monteith
H The first manned moon landing
AL A baseball mitt
SN Two
SL They musn't be too big

39
G New South Wales
E *Brookside*
H Alcohol
AL *Satanic Verses*
SN John Aspinall
SL He never did

40
G France
E Kylie Minogue
H Spain's
AL Prince Charles
SN Austria's
SL Jack Dempsey

41
G Bubonic plague
E *Strawberry Fields Forever*
H Robert Falcon Scott
AL Salman Rushdie
SN See in the dark
SL Mike Tyson

42
G Liverpool
E Lloyd Cole
H 20th Century (1909)
AL Andy Warhol
SN Fig
SL Cliff Thorburn

43
G *Disneyworld's*
E The BBC
H Conservatives
AL The Victoria and Albert
SN Jeep – (GP)
SL None

44
G Dorset
E Ronald Reagan
H Television cameras
AL Cubism
SN She came from Poland
SL Jesse Owens

45
G Blenheim Palace
E Roscoe (Fatty) Arbuckle
H *Imperial Airways*
AL Art Nouveau
SN Neptune
SL Hillsborough

46
G India
E George Gershwin
H He read it himself
AL *Labour Weekly*
SN I.K. Brunel designed Temple Meads railway station in Bristol
SL Cherries

47
G "Good Luck"
E Mike Smith
H *Jail to the chief*
AL The British Museum
SN A free eye test
SL 20

48
G Luxembourg, Liechtenstein, Lithuania and Latvia
E *Rocky*
H General Custer
AL The Louvre
SN Margaret Thatcher
SL Gin

49
G Angola
E *Spirit In the Sky*
H Britain
AL Marshall McLuhan
SN Water
SL A boar's head

50
G India's
E August
H Cruise
AL *Reader's Digest*
SN Howard Hughes
SL Hollandaise

51
G Borneo
E Boy George's
H J. F. Kennedy's
AL *A Passage to India*
SN Michael Faraday
SL Mussels

52
G French
E Warren Beatty
H France's
AL A Gutenberg Bible
SN Elements
SL The North Sea

53
G Russia's
E Sneezy
H January 15th
AL Why
SN Ammonia
SL Lentils

54
G Regent Street
E Wakefield
H 8
AL A bull and a horse
SN Butane
SL White

55
G South Africa
E 1955
H Eleven
AL The Bible
SN Three
SL A balloon

56
G Middelfart
E *Look Back In Anger*
H Geese
AL Liberace
SN The polar bear
SL Joe Mercer

Trivial Pursuit™
· G A M E 2 ·

57
G Newcastle
E Russ Conway
H Himmler
AL Elizabeth Taylor
SN Mountains
SL Bing Crosby's

58
G Tandems aren't allowed on motorways
E Holland
H Plymouth
AL Sherlock Holmes wore a deerstalker
SN Seven
SL The summit of Everest

59
G I. K. Brunel's
E Pietro Annigoni
H Henry VII
AL 1990
SN Hydrogen
SL Liverpool

60
G Bicycles
E Jamie Sommers
H The Profumo Affair
AL Tamora
SN Walks on water
SL He puts back spin on the cue ball

61
G International Youth Hostel Federation
E Supergran's
H 1970 and 1974
AL Ten years
SN No
SL Captain Becher (who gave his name to Becher's Brook)

62
G Yellow
E Moses
H One
AL Blackpool
SN Linoleum
SL Baseball

63
G Adelaide
E David Cassidy
H One
AL The National Gallery
SN Guano
SL Portsmouth

64
G Oklahoma City
E Sunday
H Sir Thomas More
AL *Pilgrim's Progress*
SN A metre
SL Jimmy White

65
G Texas
E Robbie Box
H Jeffrey Archer
AL Handel
SN Specific gravity
SL A billiards table

66
G Tom
E Cartwright
H Lord Stockton — Harold Macmillan
AL It isn't
SN Two
SL Tip-off

67
G Florence
E Mongy
H Prince Andrew
AL Westminster Abbey
SN Oil
SL Cricket

68
G Turin's
E WKRP
H The Pope
AL Ted Hughes
SN Carl Jung
SL Six

69
G The Tiber
E Wesley and Cyril
H George Bush
AL German
SN The Bull
SL Row — Oxford & Cambridge reserve ladies teams

70
G Stevenage
E Yes or No
H 19
AL Winnie the Pooh
SN A head
SL Henry Cooper appeared on *A Question of Sport*

71
G Austria's
E Tamla Motown (Detroit)
H The SAS entry into the Iranian embassy
AL *Sabre Dance*
SN A fingerprint
SL They were both goalkeepers

72
G One drachma
E Malcolm McLaren
H Fawn Hall
AL A funeral
SN Venus
SL First woman to light the Olympic flame

73
G Chopsticks
E *Discovery*
H Pol Pot
AL Bach
SN Up your nose
SL Annually

74
G Bristol
E The Queen's Christmas Day Message
H Pierre Trudeau
AL Playing tennis
SN None
SL Daley Thompson

75
G Honshu
E *Coronation Street*
H Six days!
AL Rugby
SN Earache
SL Thirteen

76
G Cairo
E *Grange Hill's*
H Oxford (bags)
AL *Private Eye*
SN It was made from ivory
SL The Pasadena Rose Bowl

77
G St Peter
E Michelle Fowler
H Both died in car crashes
AL Waverley
SN Masking agent
SL Arkle

78
G Orange
E *The Dagmar*
H Woodrow Wilson
AL Norman Tebbit
SN Lowest common denominator
SL Japan

79
G Birmingham
E Frank Sidebottom's
H Messina
AL Agatha Christie
SN Polio
SL Zola Budd

80
G Portugal
E Louis Armstrong
H Gibraltar
AL Isadora Duncan's
SN Ivan Pavlov
SL Tennis

81
G Scotland's
E Bessie Smith
H Ron Brown
AL Eliza Doolittle
SN Helen Keller
SL Roger Bannister

82
G Vesuvius
E 60th
H The London City Airport
AL Michelango
SN A computer error
SL Lloyd Honeyghan

83
G Amsterdam
E The Beatles
H Florence Nightingale
AL Barbara Hepworth
SN Quinine is obtained from the chinchona tree
SL Zola Budd

84
G Jersey
E *The Rovers Return*
H T. E. Lawrence (of Arabia)
AL Sarah Keays
SN Someone else's heart
SL Larry Holmes

85
G Westminster Abbey
E *Brookside*
H To make Edward the Duke of Windsor
AL Two
SN Force
SL Weight-lifting

86
G Three
E Churchill's funeral
H A moustache
AL *The Rose*
SN These were groups said to be most at risk from AIDS
SL Speedway

87
G Monaco and Paris
E Gordon the Gopher
H Martin Luther King
AL Lord Peter Wimsey
SN A house fly
SL 26

88
G Three years
E *Sooty*
H Ho Chi Minh
AL Sport
SN Japan
SL Chelsea

ANSWERS

89
- **G** Denmark
- **E** Freddie Starr
- **H** Pope John Paul II
- **AL** Jack the Ripper
- **SN** Five
- **SL** The Commonwealth Games

90
- **G** White
- **E** Violet Carson
- **H** Piper Alpha
- **AL** Train spotting
- **SN** The sun
- **SL** Sir Frank Worrell appears on Barbados' $5-note

91
- **G** The Palace of Westminster
- **E** Didgeridoo
- **H** Koo Stark
- **AL** Cake tin liners
- **SN** Bulb
- **SL** Moved it closer to the hole

92
- **G** Victoria
- **E** Albert Memorial Hospital
- **H** Holland
- **AL** Cecil Beaton
- **SN** Goat
- **SL** Foot and Mouth disease

93
- **G** Romulus and Remus
- **E** Roy Walker
- **H** Banana
- **AL** *Today's*
- **SN** Mercury
- **SL** The Boat Race

94
- **G** Lake Michigan
- **E** *Relative Strangers*
- **H** Shirley Williams
- **AL** 1985
- **SN** Zulu
- **SL** They both got a gold

95
- **G** York's
- **E** He delivered the mail
- **H** Margaret Thatcher
- **AL** Heads
- **SN** Twenty-two
- **SL** Playing croquet

96
- **G** Charleston, South Carolina
- **E** *L. A. Law*
- **H** Sinn Fein
- **AL** Don Quixote
- **SN** Helium
- **SL** Great Britain

97
- **G** Parma
- **E** *Acorn Antiques*
- **H** Prince Philip
- **AL** Godot
- **SN** K
- **SL** Fifth

98
- **G** The Costa del Sol
- **E** His car
- **H** Prince Philip
- **AL** The Mappa Mundi
- **SN** Trees
- **SL** The penalty

99
- **G** Damascus
- **E** Communications Officer
- **H** 1982
- **AL** Beethoven's
- **SN** Your ears
- **SL** Out first ball in both innings

100
- **G** Holland
- **E** The Larkins
- **H** Portugal
- **AL** *Funeral in Berlin*
- **SN** Tea
- **SL** Red

101
- **G** Margaret Thatcher
- **E** Mr Ed
- **H** Sark
- **AL** Verona
- **SN** A bull
- **SL** A spare

102
- **G** Alaska
- **E** *Brookside*
- **H** Two
- **AL** Defoe
- **SN** Cro-Magnon
- **SL** Primo Carnera's

103
- **G** Blue
- **E** Paul Shane
- **H** The half penny
- **AL** King Wenceslas
- **SN** Four
- **SL** Simon Le Bon's

104
- **G** *Autostrade*
- **E** Anger
- **H** Prince Harry
- **AL** The Artful Dodger
- **SN** Bit the judge
- **SL** None

105
- **G** Nottinghamshire
- **E** *I Gotta Woman*
- **H** Ho Chi Minh
- **AL** Germany
- **SN** In the brain
- **SL** Fullback

106
- **G** Denmark's
- **E** "Heil Hitler"
- **H** The Maginot Line
- **AL** New Delhi
- **SN** Duck's
- **SL** Snooker

107
- **G** Yes
- **E** Jesus
- **H** St Edward's Crown
- **AL** *Huckleberry Finn*
- **SN** The toilet
- **SL** Morse

108
- **G** The Colosseum
- **E** *The Towering Inferno*
- **H** 1990
- **AL** Music
- **SN** Henry Ford
- **SL** None

109
- **G** Japan's
- **E** Jessica Lange
- **H** *The Golden Hind*
- **AL** *La Traviata*
- **SN** Bird
- **SL** A golfer

110
- **G** Spend them
- **E** Denny Laine
- **H** Spain's
- **AL** L-Y
- **SN** Opium
- **SL** Douglas Jardine

111
- **G** Jerusalem
- **E** Genesis
- **H** The Falkland Islands
- **AL** Enid Blyton's
- **SN** Breathe
- **SL** Richie Benaud

112
- **G** Phoenix
- **E** *Always On My Mind*
- **H** India
- **AL** Sigmund Freud's
- **SN** Two
- **SL** Eight

Trivial Pursuit
·GAME 3·

113
- **G** Tom Price
- **E** Pet Shop Boys
- **H** Muslim
- **AL** *Catch 22*
- **SN** Forty
- **SL** Johnny Weissmuller

114
- **G** Luxembourg
- **E** Rocky Balboa
- **H** Prince Andrew
- **AL** *Wind in the Willows*
- **SN** Chlorofluorocarbons (CFCs)
- **SL** Giant Haystacks

115
- **G** Anglican
- **E** *Takeover Bid*
- **H** Captain Cook
- **AL** Florence
- **SN** Britain
- **SL** Backgammon

116
- **G** Glastonbury
- **E** 1925
- **H** Lech Walesa won the Nobel Peace Prize in 1983
- **AL** Sarah Bernhardt
- **SN** San Francisco
- **SL** Lester Piggott

117
- **G** Staffordshire
- **E** Not guilty
- **H** By abseiling
- **AL** Norwegian
- **SN** 1903
- **SL** Joe Di Maggio

(118)
G Tapas
E W. C. Fields
H 1901
AL Snowy
SN A cheetah's claws don't retract
SL Heysel

(119)
G Manhattan
E *Another Day In Paradise*
H G.G.
AL The Satanic Verses
SN Mercedes
SL Severe frostbite

(120)
G Dartmoor
E Bessie Street
H Margaret Hilda Roberts (Thatcher)
AL The National Gallery
SN It doesn't hold water it holds fat
SL Once

(121)
G Belgium
E *Howard's Way*
H 1921
AL Salvador Dali
SN Use C. B. radios
SL Stirling Moss

(122)
G Metropolitan
E *The Walford Chronicle*
H Kenya
AL Queen Victoria
SN The dodo
SL Cambridge

(123)
G Africa
E Peach
H The Queen's Silver Jubilee
AL Cricket
SN Blood
SL Ian Botham

(124)
G British Columbia
E *Hell's Angels*
H Prince Charles
AL *Amahl and the Night Visitors*
SN Horns
SL Wimbledon

(125)
G Three
E Termites
H By roasting
AL He only had one arm
SN Aspirin
SL Chelsea

(126)
G Orinoco
E The Federation
H George Adamson
AL Iolanthe
SN A sandstorm
SL Bad weather

(127)
G Australia
E Bully
H John Major
AL *Hamlet*
SN None
SL Snooker

(128)
G Buckinghamshire
E *Follyfoot (The Lightning Tree)*
H Ronald Reagan's
AL None of them
SN Iodine
SL Emil Zatopek

(129)
G Batman
E A two-way radio
H Tonga's
AL The jawbone of an ass
SN Black
SL The Queen

(130)
G The Inn
E The Woodentops
H Dennis Nilson
AL Harvey Smith
SN Paint their eyes
SL Royal Blackheath

(131)
G Tanzania
E *Knot's Landing*
H One thousand pounds
AL Grimm
SN None
SL Sir Stanley Matthews was the first footballer to receive a knighthood

(132)
G Truro
E Wagon Train
H Michael Heseltine
AL Limerick
SN Venus
SL Tokyo's

(133)
G Alaska
E *The Braden Beat*
H Richard Nixon
AL They were invented by a Mr Camel
SN Percolating
SL *Colemanballs*

(134)
G Bangladesh
E A 'Ripping Yarn'
H A pardon
AL Prostitutes
SN Tails
SL *Scrabble*

(135)
G Turin
E *Upstairs, Downstairs*
H USA
AL Lady Chatterley
SN Uranus
SL Tennis

(136)
G The Eiffel Tower was built for the 1889 Paris Exhibition
E *He Ain't Heavy He's My Brother*
H Ivan IV
AL The Queen
SN Wine
SL Three of a kind and a pair

(137)
G Devon
E Conway and Twitty
H Edwina Currie
AL Harry Secombe
SN Mercury
SL Danish

(138)
G North Yorkshire
E Major Houlihan was more commonly known as 'Hotlips'
H Terry Waite
AL Joan Collins
SN Pinball
SL 1928

(139)
G Venezuela
E Jimi Hendrix's
H *British Telecom* shares
AL Vincent Price
SN Butterfly
SL Shoes

(140)
G Fleet Street
E *Unchained Melody*
H Zeebrugge
AL It is the world's most venomous fish
SL Philip Noel-Baker

(141)
G Central Park
E Hinge and Bracket
H Breadfruit plants
AL Vincent Van Gogh
SN Gold
SL *Grand Marnier*

(142)
G Afghanistan
E Rubber Duck
H *H.M.S. Hermes*
AL Rosalynn Carter's
SN A guide dogs for the blind school
SL Water-skiing

(143)
G Sheep
E Norman Bates (in *Psycho*)
H Captain Hardy
AL Doric
SN Dentist
SL Seb Coe

(144)
G Moscow
E Heroin
H Abraham Lincoln
AL Roy Lichtenstein's
SN Day's eye
SL Gladitorial combats

(145)
G Big Ben
E *The Life of Brian*
H Louis XVI
AL The bull
SN Three
SL 1996

(146)
G Port Argentina
E Jamie Lee Curtis
H Avon
AL *Lace 2*
SN One-eighth
SL The pommel

(147)
G Tea
E *The Really Useful Theatre Company*
H Their blood group
AL Charles Darnay's
SN Four
SL The square dance

(148)
- **G** South Africa
- **E** *When constabulary duty's to be done*
- **H** 10
- **AL** Jesus and Mary
- **SN** The Sun
- **SL** Jimmy Carter

(149)
- **G** Mount St Helens
- **E** Edmund
- **H** Japanese Americans
- **AL** *Gulliver's Travels*
- **SN** Hazelnut
- **SL** One

(150)
- **G** Five
- **E** Marlene Dietrich
- **H** FEED THE WORLD
- **AL** Winnie-the-Pooh
- **SN** Balloon
- **SL** Bradford City

(151)
- **G** The Panama Canal's
- **E** *Death On The Rock*
- **H** Enniskillen's
- **AL** The Last Night of the Proms
- **SN** 5%
- **SL** First woman to swim the channel

(152)
- **G** New York City
- **E** Dawn and Jennifer
- **H** Gandhi
- **AL** Alexander Solzhenitsyn
- **SN** Hedgehog
- **SL** Graeme Hick

(153)
- **G** Black Red Gold
- **E** A large Scotch
- **H** The Battle of the Somme
- **AL** Rupert
- **SN** Corn
- **SL** Ten

(154)
- **G** The Netherlands
- **E** Alastair Burnet
- **H** Three
- **AL** Mark Twain
- **SN** Listeria
- **SL** Oh So Sharp

(155)
- **G** Torquay
- **E** Wales
- **H** The Yeti (Abominable Snowman)
- **AL** Mappa Mundi
- **SN** Advanced Passenger Trains
- **SL** Nigel Mansell

(156)
- **G** English
- **E** Ray Moore
- **H** Kent State University
- **AL** Golf
- **SN** Eight
- **SL** Ian Botham

(157)
- **G** Spanish
- **E** Craps
- **H** Olaf Palme
- **AL** *Here Comes the Bride*
- **SN** May
- **SL** Norway

(158)
- **G** South America
- **E** Kirsty McColl
- **H** Lockerbie
- **AL** Odo of Bayeux, half-brother to William the Conqueror, commissioned the Bayeux Tapestry
- **SN** Apollo Eleven
- **SL** The America's Cup

(159)
- **G** Calcutta
- **E** Archer
- **H** He attended two Catholic funerals
- **AL** *The Pirates of Penzance*
- **SN** The electric razor
- **SL** 1971

(160)
- **G** The Mississippi
- **E** Lovers (*The Lovers*)
- **H** The Queen Mother's
- **AL** Anthony Burgess
- **SN** July and August
- **SL** Finnish

(161)
- **G** I
- **E** Husband and wife
- **H** U.N. General Secretary
- **AL** 11th
- **SN** Pear
- **SL** The Boat Race

(162)
- **G** George II
- **E** Stoker
- **H** The SDP's Gang of Four
- **AL** William Shakespeare
- **SN** The big bang theory
- **SL** Jesse Owens

(163)
- **G** Rosetta
- **E** Sandy Richardson
- **H** Michael Fagan
- **AL** Kingsley Amis
- **SN** Ants
- **SL** Trap 6

(164)
- **G** Duchess of York (Fergie)
- **E** Number 73
- **H** Greenham Common
- **AL** Princess Diana's
- **SN** Asbestos
- **SL** Bridge

(165)
- **G** Isle of Wight's
- **E** Oy
- **H** The IRA
- **AL** A crossbow
- **SN** Maize
- **SL** Christopher

(166)
- **G** The Thames
- **E** *In space*
- **H** Neil Kinnock
- **AL** It's an embroidery
- **SN** Rainfall
- **SL** Ronald Reagan

(167)
- **G** Chicago
- **E** *Name that Tune*
- **H** Red
- **AL** A vicarage
- **SN** 12.34 and 56 seconds on 7th August 1990
- **SL** The Crucible Theatre, Sheffield

(168)
- **G** The Quarter Days
- **E** Lorne Greene
- **H** By train
- **AL** April
- **SN** The horse
- **SL** A cricket pitch

(Trivial Pursuit · GAME 4 ·)

(169)
- **G** Niagara Falls
- **E** Rumpole
- **H** Prague
- **AL** Charlie Chaplin's
- **SN** Magnesium
- **SL** 12. (6 stumps, 4 bails, 2 bats

(170)
- **G** Yorkshire Dales
- **E** British Satellite Broadcasting
- **H** Charles
- **AL** Landseer's (designer of the lions)
- **SN** The shell
- **SL** Fuel shortage

(171)
- **G** Mont Blanc
- **E** The Who
- **H** Churchill
- **AL** The book's title
- **SN** Pterodactyl
- **SL** 1990

(172)
- **G** Sheffield
- **E** Elton John
- **H** Queen Victoria
- **AL** By drowning
- **SN** Green and yellow
- **SL** 1990

(173)
- **G** A punt
- **E** The Mad Hatter
- **H** His ear
- **AL** *Love Story*
- **SN** The dolphin's
- **SL** Golden Miller

(174)
- **G** Japan
- **E** Cornwall
- **H** 1940
- **AL** William Golding
- **SN** On the moon
- **SL** Eight

(175)
- **G** London, Gatwick
- **E** James Bond
- **H** Police costumes
- **AL** Brideshead Revisited
- **SN** Change position
- **SL** The Admiral's Cup

(176)
- **G** The Jubilee Line
- **E** Commercials
- **H** W.H.Smith
- **AL** Ebenezer Scrooge
- **SN** Cocaine
- **SL** The popping crease

ANSWERS

(177)
G None
E Fly
H Three
AL Somerset Maugham
SN Cheetah
SL None. (The Games were cancelled)

(178)
G Waterloo
E Gloria
H Mark
AL Music
SN Cellophane
SL A Chinaman

(179)
G The Piccadilly Line
E Elvis Costello's
H 1982
AL Virginia Wade
SN Echo
SL A googly

(180)
G Mendips
E Creedance Clearwater Revival
H British Gas
AL One
SN Cold fronts
SL Men's discus

(181)
G The Mississippi
E Fred Astaire and Ginger Rogers'
H Monster Raving Loony
AL Noah
SN Aerodynamics
SL An ice hockey puck

(182)
G Cayenne
E *Lawrence of Arabia*
H Leaving the scene of an accident
AL Italian
SN A testicle
SL Backwards

(183)
G Australia
E The sinking of the *Titanic*
H Mary I (Mary Tudor)
AL India
SN Orange, green and purple
SL Craig Johnston

(184)
G Egypt
E *The Jungle Book*
H 1983
AL Greece
SN Mung Beans
SL Yachting; Edward Heath

(185)
G China
E *Love Story*
H Himmler was head of the Gestapo
AL When he's out
SN Metamorphic
SL Ascot

(186)
G Africa
E Bob Geldof
H Ronald Reagan
AL War
SN Eggs
SL The America's Cup

(187)
G Hawaii
E *The Sun*
H A human head
AL T.S.Eliot
SN Venus
SL Bacon

(188)
G Peru
E *A Place on Earth*
H John F. Kennedy
AL Voltaire
SN Five
SL Two

(189)
G Wellington
E Arnold Schwarzenegger
H Manfred von Richthofen. (The Red Baron)
AL William Blake's
SN *Boeing*
SL White wine and soda

(190)
G The Atlantic's
E Victoria Wood
H St.Petersburg
AL Genus
SN Space
SL Sambuca

(191)
G Lloyd George
E El Paso
H Homosexual
AL Ben Elton
SN Wattle
SL The America's Cup

(192)
G Paddington
E Hold On
H Spain
AL *David Copperfield*
SN Smelly feet
SL Walford Utd.

(193)
G Four
E John Cleese
H 15
AL E.M.Forster
SN Tin
SL The M.C.C.'s

(194)
G Greek
E Anne Boleyn
H Garden gnomes
AL Sherlock Holmes
SN On the seabed
SL Table tennis

(195)
G Madrid
E *The Protectors*
H Judge Jeffreys
AL Daphne du Maurier's
SN Worms
SL Two

(196)
G Florida
E Basil
H Jack the Ripper
AL Lace making
SN Isaac Newton
SL Cassius Clay's

(197)
G Istanbul – Europe and Asia
E Jane Wyman
H *The Guardian*
AL *Paradise Lost*
SN The cuttlefish
SL Max Baer

(198)
G Houston
E Harvey Jr
H South Korea
AL *The Fourth Protocol*
SN Hot air balloon
SL One penny

(199)
G Mount Rushmore
E Jim Bergerac
H TINA
AL *Paradise Lost*
SN One hundred
SL Rowing

(200)
G The Goodwin Sands
E Perfume
H Denis Thatcher
AL Lynn Faulds Wood
SN Michael Collins
SL Gareth Edwards

(201)
G Scotland
E The Strawbs
H Prince Charles
AL *Every Good Boy Deserves Favour*
SN Air conditioning
SL *Foster's*

(202)
G Hampshire
E Nil points in the Eurovision Song Contest
H Earl of Stockton
AL In heaven
SN Spring
SL Polo

(203)
G Australia's
E Demis Roussos
H The *Mary Rose*
AL *Yankee Doodle*
SN The atomic bomb
SL None

(204)
G Rio Grande
E Tinkerbell from *Peter Pan* is based on Marilyn Monroe
H Margaret Thatcher
AL T.S.Eliot
SN Earth
SL Ian Botham

(205)
G One pound
E Horace
H John Profumo
AL Albert Camus
SN The groove under your nose
SL Five

(206)
G Cornwall
E Mike Baldwin
H The Duke of Windsor
AL Poetry
SN Caught a salmon
SL American football (best collegiate player)

ANSWERS

207
G The Bay of Biscay
E Jim Hacker
H Epsom
AL Prince Charles
SN The sun
SL Brands Hatch

208
G Paris
E Pink Floyd
H San Francisco
AL Cecil Day Lewis
SN Neptune
(until 1999 and then
it will be Pluto)
SL The Calcutta Cup

209
G South Carolina
E T'Pau
H Ruby
AL The Old Curiosity
Shop
SN A hangover
SL White City

210
G Legoland
E Bette Davis
H The Live Aid
Concert
AL Glass
SN England
SL Zola Budd

211
G Gloucestershire
E Alex Harvey
H Jeffrey Archer gave
her two thousand
pounds
AL Havana
SN D.D.T
SL 14

212
G The Pacific Ocean
E Arnold Layne
H The Queen
AL Carla
SN Their breasts
SL Jesse Owens

213
G Ned Kelly
E *Apple Films*
H Catherine Parr
AL Chopin
SN One god
SL Lionel Richie

214
G Copenhagen
E The fish
H Paul McCartney
AL Emily Dickinson
SN The stork
SL Referee Stopped
Contest

215
G The Czech Republic
E Arthur
(Dudley Moore)
H Glencoe
AL It is both their
birthdays
SN Adobe
SL Cardial Arms Park

216
G Berlin
E The world
H Twice
AL In *The Merchant of
Venice*, Shylock
loaned Antonio
2,000 ducats
SN Two
SL The Australian
Open

217
G China
E *Ring of Bright Water*
H Spain's
AL "Tiger! Tiger!
burning bright"
SN One and a quarter
(1.25)
SL Milk

218
G Indonesia
E *Levi 501s*
H Abraham Lincoln's
AL Growing pains
SN Hopping
SL The obverse

219
G Canada
E *True*
H The shape of the
Rock of Gibraltar
AL Michael Jackson
SN Chewing gum
SL Five

220
G Uganda's
E Beckindale
H U-Thant
AL Brideshead
SN Oxygen
SL Harold Larwood

221
G Uganda
E *Andy Capp*
H Athena
AL Zenda
SN Nitrogen
SL Boxing

222
G No
E *Blackadder II*
H Nikita Kruschev
AL *Treasure Island*
SN Neptune
SL Bjorn Borg

223
G Dover
E (Dirty) Den Watts
H Tuesdays
AL The Authorised
version of the Bible
SN Catkins
SL None

224
G Chepstow
E Rhoda
H Friday
AL Twelve
SN Fourteen
SL Boxing

Trivial Pursuit
GAME 5

225
G Adelaide
E M.D
H 5p and 10p.
AL Ella
SN Lead poisoning
SL Baseball

226
G The Vatican
E Trumpton
H Lemmy
AL A donkey
SN Saturn
SL Roberto Duran

227
G Wyoming
E *The Mary Tyler
Moore Show*
H Mrs Gandhi
AL *Twelfth Night*
SN The Space Shuttle
Columbia
SL Bed and Breakfast

228
G Lithuania
E *Only Fools and
Horses*
H Margaret Thatcher
AL Minnehaha
SN France
SL Indianapolis

229
G Berkshire
E One of his teeth
H Mongolia's
AL Jane
SN Bicycles
SL The Whitbread
Gold Cup

230
G Paris
E Clocks
H Nancy Reagan
AL Mount Rushmore
SN C
SL The marathon

231
G Florida
E Tim Brooke-Taylor
H It was a horse
AL The Caine Mutiny
SN Caribou
SL Rugby

232
G The ABC Islands
E Roy Plomley
H Imelda
AL Shirley Conran's
SN Saturn
SL David Broome

233
G The Taj Mahal
E A cow
H Austin Mitchell
AL An oboe
SN *Eagle*
SL 100-1

234
G They're both called
Kensington Gore
E Guru Josh
H Ramsay
MacDonald
AL Picasso's
SN Toilet paper
SL Elvis Presley

235
G Switzerland
E Frank Sinatra
H A heatwave
AL Anna Pavlova
SN The Flying
Bedstead
SL Eddie (The Eagle)
Edwards

236
- **G** Lamb
- **E** Charlie Chaplin
- **H** The '50s
- **AL** Norwegian
- **SN** Orville Wright
- **SL** The Bodyline Tour

237
- **G** The M5
- **E** *Close Encounters of the Third Kind – Special Edition*
- **H** Josephine
- **AL** E.M.Forster's
- **SN** Marie Stopes
- **SL** The Los Angeles Olympics

238
- **G** Norwich
- **E** Tom Hark
- **H** Adolf Hitler
- **AL** Between the r and the s
- **SN** A wave
- **SL** Orienteering

239
- **G** Americans spell it c-e-n-t-e-r
- **E** *B-A-B-Y*
- **H** Julius Caesar's
- **AL** Paris
- **SN** 1910
- **SL** 400m

240
- **G** John Cleese
- **E** John Lennon
- **H** DORA
- **AL** Luciano Pavarotti
- **SN** Two
- **SL** Prince Charles

241
- **G** The Arno
- **E** *2001-A Space Odyssey*
- **H** Jesse James
- **AL** Mary Magdalene
- **SN** Tungsten
- **SL** Fifteen

242
- **G** Fifteen
- **E** *Star Trek III*
- **H** Fritz
- **AL** Mary and her little lamb
- **SN** Bats
- **SL** "Floats like a butterfly, stings like a bee"

243
- **G** Spain's
- **E** Humphrey Bogart
- **H** Paris
- **AL** Edgar Allan Poe
- **SN** Bronze
- **SL** The Marathon

244
- **G** South Africa
- **E** Channel 4
- **H** Charles Manson
- **AL** Tiny Tim
- **SN** Malaria
- **SL** Vat 69

245
- **G** The Arctic Circle
- **E** *Sgt Pepper's*
- **H** Gang of Four
- **AL** Pandora
- **SN** The lily
- **SL** 21

246
- **G** *Jack Daniels*
- **E** Abbey Road
- **H** Canada
- **AL** Sand
- **SN** A picosecond
- **SL** It gallops

247
- **G** One
- **E** Dorothy from the film *Tootsie* was played by Dustin Hoffmann
- **H** Peru
- **AL** Cyprus
- **SN** December 25th
- **SL** Twenty one

248
- **G** A lion
- **E** Arnold Schwarzenegger
- **H** The I.R.A
- **AL** Linus
- **SN** F-14
- **SL** Sixteen

249
- **G** Cape Town
- **E** *Cagney and Lacey*
- **H** Switzerland
- **AL** *The Forsyte Saga's*
- **SN** *Ford*
- **SL** Judo

250
- **G** The District Line
- **E** Brothers
- **H** The Jarrow Marchers reached London in 1936
- **AL** The crocodile bit it off
- **SN** Erasers
- **SL** Leeds Utd

251
- **G** Trains
- **E** Jessica
- **H** Three
- **AL** Fresco
- **SN** Uranium
- **SL** Maiden

252
- **G** The dragon
- **E** *Bless This House*
- **H** Lincoln
- **AL** Whether to save the life of her son or her daughter
- **SN** Twenty-two
- **SL** Joe Frazier

253
- **G** Belgrade
- **E** Mr. Sulu
- **H** Charles II
- **AL** *Blade Runner*
- **SN** The drinking straw
- **SL** 77

254
- **G** The Tigris
- **E** A snowstorm
- **H** Bob Cryer
- **AL** The Louvre
- **SN** Van Allen Belts
- **SL** Birmingham City

255
- **G** The Philippines
- **E** Rhett Butler
- **H** Spandau
- **AL** L. S. Lowry
- **SN** Magnitude
- **SL** Emerson Fittipaldi

256
- **G** Lhasa
- **E** Bobbie
- **H** Dan Quayle
- **AL** The *Mona Lisa*
- **SN** Apple Computers
- **SL** Fencing

257
- **G** Gibraltar
- **E** John Belushi
- **H** The Brandenburg Gate
- **AL** Edouard Manet's
- **SN** Teaching young children
- **SL** Brendan Foster

258
- **G** Hawaii
- **E** Obi-Wan Kenobe
- **AL** Germany
- **AL** Masterpiece
- **SN** *V1*
- **SL** Became an undertaker

259
- **G** Japan's
- **E** Elliot
- **H** 25th December
- **AL** Spanish
- **SN** Corner to corner
- **SL** *Escape to Victory*

260
- **G** Saudi Arabia
- **E** Glenn Miller
- **H** The shilling
- **AL** Sainsbury's (The Sainsbury Wing)
- **SN** Sulphuric acid
- **SL** Angelo Dundee

261
- **G** Sunderland
- **E** Dave
- **H** Peter Sutcliffe
- **AL** Roman Polanski's
- **SN** The Chernobyl No. 1 Reactor
- **SL** 200 (obviously!)

262
- **G** Auschwitz
- **E** Prince's
- **H** Communist Party
- **AL** *The Moonlight Sonata*
- **SN** Breed fish
- **SL** Synchronized swimming

263
- **G** Two
- **E** Peckham
- **H** His little head
- **AL** Remove it from his eye
- **SN** Your skin
- **SL** Jack Nicklaus

264
- **G** The Kalahari
- **E** Prince
- **H** Hitler
- **AL** *Aida*
- **SN** Truffle
- **SL** British snooker

265
- **G** Bolivia
- **E** George Michael
- **H** Iraq
- **AL** Carmen
- **SN** It has two equal sides (or angles)
- **SL** Nine pin bowling

266
- **G** The Potomac
- **E** M.C.
- **H** Viscount Linley
- **AL** Billy the Kid
- **SN** Helium
- **SL** Curling

267
- **G** Yom Kippur
- **E** Dread Zeppelin
- **H** None
- **AL** Kiri Te Kanawa
- **SN** Black panther
- **SL** Manuel Santana

268
- **G** Intourist
- **E** *Silhouettes*
- **H** Nine
- **AL** Oscar Wilde
- **SN** Sycamore
- **SL** 1982

269
- **G** Tower Bridge
- **E** *The Singing Detective*
- **H** Africa
- **AL** Postman Pat
- **SN** The Barringer Crater
- **SL** Jack Dempsey

270
- **G** Australia
- **E** Michael Keaton
- **H** Dunkirk
- **AL** Glasgow
- **SN** The Doppler Effect
- **SL** Prince Charles

271
- **G** The Isle of Man
- **E** *EastEnders*
- **H** Winston Churchill
- **AL** Vivaldi's
- **SN** A primrose
- **SL** Halifax

272
- **G** The Rockies
- **E** The back of your hand
- **H** Transport and General Workers
- **AL** The Cheshire Cat – his smile is the last thing to disappear
- **SN** An equal and opposite reaction
- **SL** 1956

273
- **G** 071
- **E** *California Dreamin'*
- **H** Andrei Sakharov
- **AL** Madam Butterfly
- **SN** Your body
- **SL** Fulham's Craven Cottage

274
- **G** Spain
- **E** Connie Francis
- **H** King's Cross
- **AL** A box of teabags
- **SN** 1990
- **SL** Jack Dempsey

275
- **G** Delhi
- **E** Nick Berry
- **H** Ronald Reagan
- **AL** Oedipus
- **SN** Saturn
- **SL** *Monopoly*

276
- **G** Rio de Janeiro's
- **E** Terry McCann (Minder)
- **H** Sir Anthony Meyer
- **AL** Lino
- **SN** Pluto
- **SL** 50

277
- **G** Helsinki
- **E** *Gigi*
- **H** Sunday collections
- **AL** Turpentine
- **SN** Venus's
- **SL** Carriage driving

278
- **G** Pacific
- **E** Florida
- **H** Alexandria
- **AL** *Born Free*
- **SN** The beaver
- **SL** Catamarans

279
- **G** Gibraltar
- **E** Tracy Ullman
- **H** Elizabeth II
- **AL** T.S. Eliot's
- **SN** The little finger
- **SL** He is neither American nor amateur

280
- **G** Memphis
- **E** Rock Hudson
- **H** A dog (His guide dog)
- **AL** August
- **SN** The turkey
- **SL** *The Loneliness of the Long Distance Runner*

Trivial Pursuit™
• GAME 6 •

281
- **G** Athens
- **E** Las Vegas
- **H** The Cold War
- **AL** L. S. Lowry
- **SN** Edwin (Buzz) Aldrin
- **SL** Joe Frazier

282
- **G** Switzerland
- **E** *Sorry*
- **H** Peter Sutcliffe (Yorkshire Ripper)
- **AL** Two of them
- **SN** Hydrogen
- **SL** Richard Nixon

283
- **G** Winston Churchill's
- **E** Paul Simon's
- **H** Bobby Kennedy
- **AL** *Ben Hur*
- **SN** Photosynthesis
- **SL** Ted Dexter

284
- **G** Channel Islands
- **E** *Howard's Way's*
- **H** For Valour
- **AL** Florence
- **SN** None
- **SL** Roger Bannister was the first man to run a mile in under 4 minutes

285
- **G** Kampuchea
- **E** Tin Man in *The Wizard of Oz*
- **H** Harrier
- **AL** Hieroglyphics
- **SN** Tuna
- **SL** The high jump

286
- **G** Istanbul
- **E** He's one of the Flying Doctors
- **H** Joseph Stalin
- **AL** *Fido (fidore)*
- **SN** Mulch
- **SL** *Perrier*

287
- **G** Austria
- **E** *Come Dancing*
- **H** Henry VII was the first of the Tudors
- **AL** Crossword puzzles
- **SN** Green
- **SL** Sixteen

288
- **G** Dover
- **E** Angie Watts
- **H** Nine
- **AL** *Rolls-Royce* cars
- **SN** Birds
- **SL** A dead heat

289
- **G** Tulle
- **E** *Fawlty Towers*
- **H** 1960s
- **AL** Captain Flint
- **SN** Fleas
- **SL** Maureen (Little Mo) Connolly

290
- **G** Niagara Falls
- **E** It was still called *Wogan*
- **H** Nineteenth
- **AL** Pottery
- **SN** A dead one
- **SL** Pool's

291
- **G** Key West
- **E** Diane Keen
- **H** Enoch Powell
- **AL** Mr Bumble in *Oliver Twist*
- **SN** Nectarine
- **SL** It doesn't

292
- **G** St. Kitts
- **E** Selina Scott
- **H** Blackfriars
- **AL** 1000
- **SN** Dye
- **SL** On the Isle of Man

293
- **G** Strawberry Fields
- **E** Antiques
- **H** David Steel
- **AL** They were both snuff takers
- **SN** Francis Bacon
- **SL** Paul Newman

294
- **G** Seven
- **E** Nigel Planer
- **H** 1966
- **AL** Handel
- **SN** Red and green
- **SL** Goal difference

295
- G The Danube
- E Jim Bergerac
- H Syphilis
- AL Petra
- SN Twelve
- SL Peter May

296
- G A new town
- E Elton John
- H New York
- AL *The Eroica*
- SN Salmon
- SL A springboard

297
- G Arizona
- E *Chorus Line*
- H George Bush
- AL Victor Hugo's
- SN A sundial
- SL Four

298
- G Greenland's
- E Andrew Lloyd Webber
- H Pakistan's
- AL She's dumb
- SN Fossils
- SL 170

299
- G Oxfordshire
- E Ken Dodd
- H Edward Heath
- AL Icarus
- SN The ears
- SL Diego Maradona

300
- G Europe
- E *Hair*
- H His ear
- AL Boxing
- SN Four
- SL Wimbledon

301
- G France's
- E Henry
- H The Methodist Church
- AL Thomas the Tank Engine
- SN Two
- SL Arnold Schwarzenegger

302
- G Tin Pan Alley
- E Phil Lynott
- H Theodore Roosevelt
- AL Sir Stanley Spencer
- SN B2
- SL Calgary

303
- G The Czech Republic
- E Bob Geldof
- H Turkey
- AL *Chopsticks*
- SN Coca-Cola
- SL James J. Corbett

304
- G Florida
- E J. R. Hartley
- H Abraham
- AL Dresden's
- SN Rain
- SL Ashbourne

305
- G A glass of beer
- E *The Bill*
- H Five thousand pounds
- AL Jeffrey Archer
- SN Medicine
- SL Becher's Brook at Aintree

306
- G English
- E The RAF
- H A brothel
- AL Margaret Thatcher
- SN *Calypso*
- SL The Commonwealth Games

307
- G Byzantium
- E Janet
- H Sidney Street
- AL Van Gogh's
- SN Its testicles
- SL Princess Anne

308
- G Amritsar
- E Princess Grace of Monaco
- H He divorced them
- AL Nancy Mitford
- SN Jodrell Bank
- SL Mike Gatting

309
- G Ayers Rock
- E Elvis Presley
- H Madame Pompadour
- AL John Galsworthy
- SN Brian Trubshaw
- SL USA

310
- G Breakfast
- E The tango
- H The Abortion Bill
- AL Paul Gauguin
- SN By balloon
- SL Don Bradman

311
- G Lebanon
- E *Don't Leave Me This Way*
- H Geraldine Ferraro
- AL Confucius
- SN The Year of the Tiger
- SL The hands

312
- G Bolivia's
- E Kathy
- H Bobby Sands
- AL Bizet
- SN Self-raising flour
- SL The 1971 Championship was held at the end of 1970

313
- G Mongolia
- E "I'm getting married in the morning"
- H The Coronation of George VI
- AL Cynthia Payne's
- SN Tony Soper
- SL Adrian Moorhouse

314
- G The Tamar
- E Little John
- H Dysentery
- AL Salman Rushdie, *Midnight's Children*
- SN Writing
- SL 7

315
- G South Dakota
- E "I'm coming"
- H France
- AL Dante
- SN Work
- SL Fifteen

316
- G Russia's
- E Jodie Foster
- H Nine
- AL The Spanish Civil War
- SN Chi-chi the giant panda
- SL Ian Botham

317
- G Sweden's
- E The Vipers
- H Band Aid
- AL *Peter Pan*
- SN Budgerigar
- SL Argentina

318
- G Unilateral Declaration of Independence
- E Mae West
- H Tintagel
- AL *Dubliners*
- SN Piltdown
- SL Iran's

319
- G The Hudson
- E *Tutti Frutti*
- H President of the USA
- AL She's an opera singer
- SN None
- SL Darts

320
- G Three
- E Max Headroom
- H Princess Anne
- AL Agatha Christie's
- SN Jupiter's
- SL Birmingham

321
- G Dorset
- E A lion
- H Ronald Reagan
- AL *Sleeping Beauty*
- SN Men
- SL Parc des Princes

322
- G The Channel Islands
- E Jason King
- H *The Sun*
- AL Margaret Thatcher
- SN Vitamins
- SL They never leave London

323
- G The M1
- E *Basildon Bond*
- H Red Indians
- AL Terrence Rattigan
- SN Charles Darwin
- SL Darts (throwing distance)

324
- G E
- E *The Wacky Races*
- H Ronald Reagan
- AL *The Piper at the Gates of Dawn*
- SN Carbon dioxide's
- SL Struck by lightning

325
G It's a railway tunnel
E 'Allo 'Allo
H Friday
AL Carnegie Hall
SN April
SL Thailand's

326
G Bondi Beach
E Michael Caine's
H Charles Lindbergh
AL His ears
SN Nymphomania
SL 10,000

327
G South Island
E Hero
H 1900
AL Atlantis
SN Chernobyl
SL Muhammad Ali's

328
G Venezuela
E Fay Wray's most famous acting role involved screaming loudly whilst being held by King Kong
H Jehovah's Witnesses
AL Daffodils
SN Neptune
SL Vine leaves

329
G Rome
E John Lennon's
H The Gold Standard
AL Hamlet
SN Water (by spitting)
SL Badminton

330
G Monaco
E She is deaf
H Manila's
AL Nancy Mitford
SN Palm
SL *America*

331
G British Columbia
E Rod Stewart
H Cold War
AL *Portnoy's Complaint*
SN Sight
SL The British Open

332
G Mali
E *On the Waterfront*
H Charles de Gaulle's
AL Gamesmanship
SN The paint roller
SL He scored two goals – one for each team!

333
G Andes
E Carlo Ponti
H President Nasser
AL Cricket
SN In the spine
SL Ben Johnson

334
G Royal Berkshire
E *The Gentle Touch*
H Harold Macmillan
AL The Bible
SN Wedgwood
SL Mike Harding

335
G Sudan
E Fox FM
H Thirteen
AL Two
SN Nocturnal
SL Dr. W. G. Grace

336
G Put it back 24 hours
E Tina Turner
H Pancho
AL *News on Sunday*
SN Orang-utan's
SL The Derby

Trivial Pursuit™
·GAME 7·

337
G Disneyland
E Jerusalem
H Strangeways, Manchester
AL The Palace Theatre
SN The Forth Bridge
SL Bryan Robson

338
G Auckland
E 5
H 1987
AL Toulouse-Lautrec
SN 100th
SL Eusebio – he scored 9 goals

339
G Alaska
E They've all won the Eurovision Song Contest
H Five
AL Campanile
SN 18
SL 1964

340
G Four
E Prince
H Brighton
AL Hugh Heffner
SN Clockwise
SL Gary Player

341
G Seven
E Weatherfield
H The Duke of Kent
AL Tennyson
SN The swan
SL Mike Gatting

342
G Wensleydale
E *Blue Suede Shoes*
H Holt
AL *Swan Lake*
SN Birds
SL Richard Hadlee (in 1990)

343
G Andalucia
E The Prudes
H The *Titanic*
AL A Christmas card
SN Buddleia
SL St Andrews

344
G Kenya
E Hugh Cornwell
H Coal miner
AL Grandma Moses
SN Cross-eyed
SL The Princess Royal

345
G Central Park
E Andrew Lloyd Webber
H Barbara Cartland
AL *Treasure Island*
SN Thalidomide
SL Viv Richards

346
G Detroit
E Johnny Morris
H Mrs Marcos's
AL Toe
SN Emerald
SL Colin Cowdrey

347
G Liberia
E Europe
H Ken Livingstone
AL Verdi's
SN 7 million
SL Andrew Irvine

348
G North Korea's
E *Jaws*
H The *QEII*
AL Nick
SN Pierre and Marie Curie's
SL Proof

349
G Berne
E Robin
H None
AL The Beatles
SN Cannibals
SL 12

350
G Tunisia
E Warmington-on-Sea
H Jimmy Carter
AL *The Independent*
SN The lie detector
SL Won a race

351
G Only England
E Nerys Hughes
H Einstein
AL Charles Dickens is buried in Westminster Abbey
SN J
SL Four

352
G Chile
E Danny Kaye
H One
AL *Little Lord Fauntleroy*
SN The road
SL Synchronised swimming

353
G Libya
E *Soap*
H Lee Harvey Oswald
AL Batman's
SN The Soviet Union
SL Lee Trevino

354
- G: Sinhalese
- E: Dylan Thomas
- H: Rubber
- AL: Gerald Scarfe's
- SN: Blackheads
- SL: "Because it's there"

355
- G: Key West, Florida
- E: Lord Chalfont
- H: Jim Jones
- AL: Batwoman
- SN: Canada
- SL: Shergar

356
- G: Pitcairn Island
- E: *American Pie*
- H: Winston Churchill
- AL: Christopher Robin Milne
- SN: Catheter
- SL: Bowls

357
- G: Sardinia
- E: Spain
- H: Dwight D. Eisenhower
- AL: The banana
- SN: To lower the temperature
- SL: John Arlott

358
- G: Coffee
- E: *Airplane II – The Sequel*
- H: A horse (Lady Godiva)
- AL: Miss Havisham
- SN: Black and white
- SL: Seven pounds

359
- G: Monaco
- E: St Francis of Assisi's
- H: Carnac
- AL: Mr Hyde
- SN: Beer
- SL: Ian Botham

360
- G: Switzerland
- E: An even break
- H: 80,000
- AL: Dr Doolittle
- SN: Your tongue
- SL: The Greyhound Derby

361
- G: Spain and Gibraltar
- E: *Pinocchio*
- H: West Germany
- AL: One hundred
- SN: Christopher Columbus
- SL: Nadia Comaneci

362
- G: It is not in a state
- E: Steve McQueen
- H: Mark Thatcher in the Sahara desert
- AL: David Copperfield's
- SN: The rat
- SL: George Foreman

363
- G: Japan
- E: The Fairy Godmother
- H: 1984-85
- AL: *Death in Venice*
- SN: Yes
- SL: David Bryant

364
- G: Vermicelli
- E: *Silhouettes*
- H: Ronald Reagan
- AL: Furniture
- SN: Organic chemistry
- SL: Carl Lewis

365
- G: 65 million
- E: *Gibson*
- H: Chinese
- AL: Christ's face
- SN: A parsec
- SL: 800 metres

366
- G: Aachen
- E: *Jailhouse Rock*
- H: George IV's
- AL: Slip
- SN: Taurus is also known as The Bull
- SL: American football

367
- G: Devon
- E: Elvis Presley
- H: Anna Ford
- AL: Marat
- SN: Chewing
- SL: 7

368
- G: Spain
- E: Elvis Presley's
- H: One
- AL: A rug or carpet
- SN: The wrist
- SL: A wedge of lime

369
- G: Kansas'
- E: *All Shook Up*
- H: The Florin
- AL: Carl Davis
- SN: The Ides
- SL: Tequila

370
- G: The lotus
- E: Paul McCartney
- H: W. C. Fields
- AL: *The Color Purple*
- SN: Ruby
- SL: Rod Laver

371
- G: Albania's
- E: Sid Vicious
- H: Her mother
- AL: Andy Warhol
- SN: 1.5 volts
- SL: Pigeons

372
- G: A schilling
- E: 1957
- H: Boiled the flesh off the bones
- AL: "Thou shalt commit adultery"
- SN: The revolving door
- SL: Europe's leading goal scorer

373
- G: Kampuchea
- E: The Rovers Return
- H: European Currency Unit
- AL: "Evil to Him Who Evil Thinks"
- SN: Dandruff
- SL: Jocky Wilson

374
- G: Graceland
- E: Noel Edmonds
- H: James Callaghan
- AL: "My God and My Right"
- SN: Its abdomen
- SL: Chris Brasher

375
- G: England
- E: *Fame*
- H: The American Civil War
- AL: Pandemonium
- SN: Amethyst (It doesn't work!)
- SL: Howard Winstone

376
- G: Hampton Court
- E: *The Ying Tong Song*
- H: The TUC
- AL: Pope John Paul I
- SN: A
- SL: John

377
- G: Kermit
- E: Ann-Margret
- H: Spiro Agnew
- AL: Heaven
- SN: Marconi
- SL: New York Yankees

378
- G: Prince Charles
- E: Andy Peebles
- H: Cynthia Payne
- AL: *Macbeth*
- SN: Snapdragons
- SL: Steve Cram

379
- G: St. James' Palace's
- E: David Jacobs
- H: Beirut
- AL: Theatre Royal
- SN: Eating strawberries
- SL: Kathy Cook

380
- G: Devil's Island
- E: Herb Alpert
- H: Sir Christopher Wren
- AL: The restaurant
- SN: Africa
- SL: Richard Nixon

381
- G: Indian
- E: Peter Frampton
- H: France
- AL: Rubens'
- SN: 707
- SL: Golf

382
- G: Realtor
- E: *Record Mirror*
- H: Iced Tea
- AL: Fanshaw
- SN: Lamborghini specialised in tractor manufacturing
- SL: The previous cup had been stolen

383
- G: Burma's
- E: *Back to the Future*
- H: Labour
- AL: Private eye
- SN: Trees
- SL: Clay

384
- G Cambridge
- E *See You Later Tonight*
- H Clement Atlee
- AL New Orleans
- SN Assaying
- SL Oxford

385
- G Cape Horn
- E Harlow's
- H Furs
- AL *The Picture of Dorian Gray*
- SN Horsehair
- SL His collar bone (the first injury)

386
- G Belgium
- E Mrs. Dale
- H Asquith
- AL Spring
- SN Carotene
- SL Manchester United

387
- G A wall
- E Jade
- H Liberal
- AL Brutus
- SN A chromosome
- SL Liverpool

388
- G It is the world's largest National Park
- E *An American Tail*
- H The Symbionese Liberation Army
- AL Customers had to have the horse nearest the door
- SN Their teeth
- SL Japan

389
- G Iceland
- E *Aliens*
- H Bronze Age
- AL Exmoor
- SN Husband
- SL Wedge

390
- G Capri
- E *Concorde*
- H Hoover
- AL David Copperfield
- SN 1000
- SL Three

391
- G The Tamar
- E The Bluebell Girls
- H Papyrus
- AL Brother and sister
- SN Excrement
- SL Boxing

392
- G German
- E *Son of My Father*
- H Beijing
- AL Vincent Van Gogh
- SN Bursitis
- SL The Soviet Union

Trivial Pursuit
·G A M E 8·

393
- G Water
- E Judy Collins
- H Simon de Montfort
- AL Haworth was the first home of The Brontë sisters
- SN The elder
- SL Yes

394
- G The Severn Estuary
- E Chas and Dave
- H Robert Kennedy
- AL *Twelfth Night*
- SN The sperm whale
- SL London Welsh

395
- G Cambridge's
- E Richard Pryor
- H 1957
- AL *Hello Dolly*
- SN The gazelle
- SL Bob Fitzsimmons

396
- G Zimbabwe
- E *Blake's 7*
- H Twenty
- AL White
- SN It raises the heart rate
- SL Linford Christie

397
- G The Smithsonian Institute
- E Leslie Grantham
- H Trotsky
- AL J.R.R. Tolkien's
- SN He invented the metronome
- SL Eight feet

398
- G The Atlantic
- E Pat Sharp
- H Zambia
- AL Scarlett O'Hara
- SN Permafrost
- SL Peter Scudamore

399
- G Police-(Gendarmes are military with civil duties)
- E Dennis Waterman
- H 2
- AL The Admiral Benbow
- SN Copper
- SL Checkers

400
- G Melbourne
- E Greendale (in *Postman Pat*)
- H Houston
- AL Benjamin Disraeli's
- SN Hairs
- SL Williams (J.P.R.)

401
- G Thailand
- E They are brothers
- H Thanksgiving
- AL Michelangelo's
- SN Eyes
- SL England

402
- G Geneva
- E Del Boy's
- H 1961
- AL Robert Maxwell
- SN A sperm bank
- SL Red

403
- G Mount McKinley
- E Eliot Ness
- H Two
- AL London
- SN Economics
- SL 30

404
- G Indonesia
- E *Three Men and a Baby*
- H Fidel Castro
- AL The Pied Piper
- SN An eye test chart
- SL Norwich City

405
- G Canada
- E *The Lady in Red*
- H Windsor
- AL Women's hosiery
- SN Black
- SL Behind the ball

406
- G Sumatra
- E Superboy
- H Abraham Lincoln
- AL Wynken, Blynken and Nod
- SN 15
- SL New Zealand

407
- G Darwin
- E Their Eurovision Song Contest entry
- H Yvonne Fletcher
- AL Merde (shit)
- SN Four
- SL Brian London

408
- G Vienna
- E Ram
- H Marco Polo
- AL Barbara Hepworth
- SN The Biblical
- SL Nick Faldo

409
- G USA
- E *The Inn of the Sixth Happiness*
- H Greece
- AL Mold
- SN The brain
- SL Sharron Davies

410
- G Liberia
- E Jeff Bridges
- H Alexander the Great
- AL Quasimodo
- SN Your own body
- SL Cycling

411
- G Victoria and Tasmania
- E Calypso
- H Elizabeth I
- AL *Othello*
- SN Primates
- SL Slow

412
- G Toronto's
- E Robin Hood
- H Princess Diana
- AL Humpty Dumpty
- SN A domesticated dog
- SL Donald Budge

ANSWERS

413
G Cuba
E Jack Nicholson
H 35
AL *Trial by Jury*
SN A leek
SL Newmarket

414
G Preston
E World War I
H Four
AL Wine
SN The tulip
SL Nine

415
G Canals
E Liberty Valance
H 18th
AL Two meanings
SN 37
SL Santa Claus

416
G Madagascar
E Goldfinger
H M.P.s
AL Castor and Pollux
SN Shoes
SL Stanley Matthews

417
G Cairo
E Chicago
H St. Augustine
AL The Roman
  Catholic Church
SN *Spinal Tap*
SL Cheltenham

418
G The bride
E Martha
H British
  Expeditionary
  Force
AL *You Only Live Twice*
SN Earth
SL Three

419
G The Black Sea
E Cooking
H Rudolf Hess was
  imprisoned in
  Spandau
AL La Mancha
SN Chemical weapons
SL A palm tree

420
G Tangier
E *M*A*S*H*
H 1969
AL Andy Warhol
SN None
SL In the bullpen

421
G Edelweiss
E Pat Phoenix
H Charles II
AL Four
SN Vitamin A
SL The Indianapolis
  500

422
G Crusoe found
  Friday
E Nugent
H Nelson Mandela
AL Van Gogh's
SN Dropped it
SL Four

423
G Everest
E *Busman's Holiday*
H Ronald Reagan
AL Three
SN Nuclear
  submarines
SL Manchester United

424
G Denmark
E Esther Williams
H Caroline
AL Thunder
SN A sheep
SL A head butt

425
G Majorca
E *Mickey*
H Reagan and Bush
AL Esmeralda
SN The Antarctic
SL One minute

426
G Bermuda
E Walt Disney
H George III was
  known as 'Farmer
  George'
AL Thursday's
SN The dormouse
SL Mark Spitz

427
G Canterbury
  Cathedral's
E Bob Marley's
H South Africa
AL Uillean pipes
SN Cortisone
SL 32

428
G A Samovar
E *(The Club) At the
  End of the Street*
H The Hilton
AL *Barbarella*
SN Insulin
SL Denis Law

429
G Lincolnshire
E Prince Edward
H Francis Bacon
AL *A Winter's Tale*
SN Liquid Oxygen
SL Bastard

430
G India
E *Puttin' On The Ritz*
H Lee Harvey Oswald
AL Fra Angelico
SN Lily
SL Seb Coe

431
G China
E Laurence Olivier
H Henry II
AL The pig
SN The kiwi's
SL Train

432
G Black
E Elvis Presley
H Anwar Sadat
AL The turkey
SN Black
SL Preston North End

433
G The Spanish
  National Anthem
  has no words
E Barbra Streisand
H 2nd century AD
AL *1984*
SN A chicken
SL The 1930s

434
G The Vatican
E Richard Williams
H 19th
AL Tom Jones
SN Yes
SL Shot putt

435
G French
E *Two of a Kind*
H Leader
AL Eighteen
SN Pearls
SL Pakistan

436
G China
E Blake Edwards
H The Great Wall of
  China
AL Ayesha
SN One
SL The marathon

437
G Idaho
E Bo Derek
H Constantine
AL *The Railway
  Children*
SN Wheat
SL Derek Hatton

438
G Blackpool's
E The Tin Man
H 20th Century
AL The Minotaur
SN The sole of the foot
SL Yellow

439
G Ankara
E Mel Blanc
H Alexander III
AL Broth without any
  bread
SN Sixty
SL Peter Shilton

440
G Ireland's
E *Heineken*
H Cunard's
AL *Henry VIII*
SN Cactus
SL Lester Piggott

441
G California
E *Charlie's Angels*
H Mick Jagger
AL Daphne du Maurier
SN Five
SL The Earl of Derby

442
G Mayonnaise
E *M*A*S*H's*
H Jess Yates
AL Four
SN Royal Jelly
SL Scotland

443
G Four
E Burt Bacharach
H Prince Philip
AL Figaro
SN Green
SL Frank Bruno

444
G Gillie
E Harry
H The Big Bang
AL Eggshells
SN Your wrist
SL John Spencer

445
G The Punjab
E Foghorn Leghorn's
H France
AL *The Observer*
SN A hare
SL The Queen

446
G Scotland
E *La Bamba*
H Eight
AL Mrs. Beeton's
SN Blue
SL Mark Spitz

447
G Mason-Dixon Line
E Two
H Corsica, Elba and St. Helena
AL Salman Rushdie's *Satanic Verses*
SN Green
SL Six

448
G The US Dollar
E *Motown*
H P.W. Botha
AL Moslem
SN Fish fins
SL Two over par

Trivial Pursuit
·GAME 9·

449
G Boston
E The Scarecrow
H Adolf Hitler
AL *The Barber of Seville*
SN It is born
SL Arthur

450
G Sweden
E *Batman*
H Britain's first supermarket
AL M
SN The thorax
SL Harry Carpenter

451
G Bury St. Edmunds
E Greta Garbo's
H The Korean War
AL *Animal Farm*
SN 8 kilometres per hour
SL Pele

452
G Popocatepetl
E *The Joker*
H Richard II
AL A strawberry
SN A parabola
SL Badminton

453
G A snake
E *Walk On The Wild Side* — Lou Reed
H Seven
AL Isadora Duncan was strangled after her scarf got caught in the wheel of a moving car
SN Amethyst
SL Fifteen miles per hour

454
G Sugar
E Cliff Richard
H The Battle of Crécy
AL Moliére
SN Yes
SL Name the dog that found the World Cup

455
G Malaysia
E Stevie Wonder
H Muslim
AL Round
SN California (californium)
SL *McDonald's*

456
G Malawi
E *The First Time Ever I Saw Your Face*
H Scotland's
AL Sir Jacob Epstein
SN A right leg
SL Yes

457
G The peso
E Charlie Chaplin
H Walter Cronkite
AL Abstract
SN Rose
SL The cycle road race

458
G Panama
E Shirley Temple
H John F. Kennedy
AL Dustin Hoffman
SN A codling
SL Ben Johnson

459
G Christopher Columbus
E *Gone With the Wind*
H The Mafia
AL Michael Palin
SN Cocks and hens
SL There is at least one of the colours in every national flag.

460
G Toronto's
E Five
H Margaret Thatcher
AL Samuel Beckett
SN It uncurls
SL China

461
G 8 (8848)
E Mae West
H Kentucky
AL Rachmaninov
SN Mars
SL Bean curd

462
G Simon Bolivar
E Martin Sheen
H Social Democratic Party
AL Atlas
SN Fuchsia
SL Canada

463
G China
E Prince's
H Protestant
AL Edward Lear's
SN Cathode
SL The Oval

464
G Lincolnshire
E Kenneth Williams
H Duke
AL It was based in Cambridge Circus
SN The falcon
SL Lacrosse

465
G Loch Ness
E Plasterer
H Cary Grant
AL George Smiley
SN The kestrel
SL White

466
G Venezuela's
E Baker
H Australia and Antarctica
AL Ian Fleming's
SN Raspberry pips
SL His toes

467
G July
E Victoria Wood
H Martin Luther King
AL Welsh
SN An antelope would be jumping
SL Gymnastics

468
G New Zealand
E Led Zeppelin's
H Henry Ford
AL *Zorba the Greek*
SN Cat's whiskers
SL The Manhattan

469
G Maryland
E Britt Ekland
H Four
AL "All the world's a stage"
SN One
SL Flowers

470
G Ferdinand Magellan
E *Dear Prudence*
H Prince Philip
AL Dada
SN A whale
SL American Football

471
G The Canton
E Samantha Fox
H William III
AL Ivor Novello
SN Wilhelm Roentgen
SL East Germany

472
- **G** Napoleon
- **E** Linda McCartney
- **H** 1973
- **AL** Bram Stoker
- **SN** Strong lagers
- **SL** Middleweight

473
- **G** Lake Victoria
- **E** Z.Z. Top
- **H** French
- **AL** Oscar Wilde
- **SN** Low blood pressure
- **SL** The 1st Olympic Games

474
- **G** Denmark
- **E** *The Spotty Dog*
- **H** Alec Douglas-Home
- **AL** Tarzan
- **SN** Barbara Woodhouse
- **SL** Haggis Hurling

475
- **G** Hyde Park
- **E** Paul Newman's
- **H** The Pony Express
- **AL** *Romeo and Juliet*
- **SN** Ribs
- **SL** Mayfair

476
- **G** Blue
- **E** Stewart Copeland
- **H** Twelve
- **AL** An author
- **SN** Able
- **SL** Guns

477
- **G** France
- **E** *Purple Rain*
- **H** Dickie Byrd
- **AL** Kanga
- **SN** Edison
- **SL** Beans

478
- **G** Karachi
- **E** *Buddy Can You Spare A Dime*
- **H** Charles Haughey
- **AL** China's
- **SN** Lead
- **SL** Gold

479
- **G** The River Dixence
- **E** Sid Vicious was in Siouxie and the Banshees
- **H** The English Civil War
- **AL** "Drink Me"
- **SN** Tan or light brown
- **SL** Sweet wine

480
- **G** Botswana
- **E** *The Colour of Money*
- **H** The French Foreign Legion
- **AL** Miss Marple
- **SN** Your blood pressure
- **SL** *Kronenbourg's*

481
- **G** Milan
- **E** *Animal Crackers*
- **H** Golden (50th)
- **AL** Abraham
- **SN** Iridium
- **SL** Female

482
- **G** Maelstrom
- **E** Lofty
- **H** The gun he shot Lee Harvey Oswald with
- **AL** Leonardo da Vinci
- **SN** The seashore
- **SL** Malcolm Campbell

483
- **G** Caen
- **E** Madness
- **H** Fly into space
- **AL** J.M. Barrie's
- **SN** A duck
- **SL** Australian

484
- **G** China's
- **E** Michael Jackson
- **H** Benito Mussolini was known in Italy as 'Il Duce'
- **AL** William Blake
- **SN** A plum
- **SL** He wasn't — it was taken off him

485
- **G** Amsterdam is the home of Van der Valk
- **E** *A Chorus Line*
- **H** None
- **AL** P-A-J-A-M-A-S
- **SN** Apple tree
- **SL** Long jump

486
- **G** Borneo
- **E** Acid House parties
- **H** 16 hours
- **AL** Sunday's child
- **SN** *Star Trek's*
- **SL** Arsenal

487
- **G** Paraguay
- **E** Paul McCartney
- **H** *Teenage Mutant Ninja Turtles*
- **AL** Brother
- **SN** Their hands
- **SL** Eight

488
- **G** Nicosia
- **E** *Jealous Guy*
- **H** Napoleon
- **AL** Napoleon
- **SN** Period pains
- **SL** A cricket ball

489
- **G** Boomerangs
- **E** Kid Creole
- **H** World War II
- **AL** *Inferno*
- **SN** On your cold sores
- **SL** Niki Lauda

490
- **G** Stockholm
- **E** A handkerchief. (He also had a shave that day!)
- **H** *The Sunday Correspondent*
- **AL** A pendulum clock
- **SN** Flippers
- **SL** West Ham United

491
- **G** Zaire
- **E** Graham Chapman
- **H** Ponies
- **AL** Marilyn Monroe
- **SN** Karl Benz
- **SL** He was the first million pound goalkeeper

492
- **G** Vodka
- **E** West Jamaica
- **H** Angela Rippon
- **AL** Garlic
- **SN** Five
- **SL** Millwall

493
- **G** British Honduras
- **E** Bette Davis
- **H** Queen Anne
- **AL** *As You Like It*
- **SN** The I.Q. Test
- **SL** Candy

494
- **G** The United Arab Emirates
- **E** John Belushi
- **H** Charles I
- **AL** *Cinderella*
- **SN** Gold
- **SL** Twenty-two

495
- **G** Lahore
- **E** *Tubular Bells*
- **H** Fifteenth
- **AL** Dance Hall
- **SN** The rabbit's
- **SL** Saffron

496
- **G** English
- **E** Elton John
- **H** Scotland
- **AL** Harry Wharton
- **SN** Alcohol
- **SL** The British Open

497
- **G** San Marino
- **E** *Wide Eyed And Legless*
- **H** Spain
- **AL** Spanish
- **SN** Above
- **SL** A neutral corner

498
- **G** Freetown
- **E** Saxophone
- **H** Christopher Columbus
- **AL** Helen of Troy's
- **SN** A tangerine
- **SL** Marsala

499
- **G** Sweden
- **E** The skunk
- **H** Henry VIII
- **AL** Venice
- **SN** The genitals
- **SL** The knight

500
- **G** Ontario
- **E** *Roxanne*
- **H** The Norman Conquest
- **AL** Art Nouveau
- **SN** Copper
- **SL** Tennis

501
- **G** A department store
- **E** Six
- **H** Winchester
- **AL** Pop Art
- **SN** Tin and lead
- **SL** Liechtenstein

502
- **G** Rome
- **E** Avon
- **H** Philadelphia
- **AL** Picasso
- **SN** Electricity
- **SL** Wraps stone

503
- **G** The Ukraine
- **E** Bing Crosby
- **H** Air Minister
- **AL** Vincent Van Gogh
- **SN** One each
- **SL** Miami

504
- **G** The United Kingdom
- **E** Kiss
- **H** Archbishop of Canterbury
- **AL** Giotto
- **SN** Amino acids
- **SL** Puissance

Trivial Pursuit
· GAME 10 ·

505
- **G** Corfu
- **E** Her broomstick
- **H** John Paul I
- **AL** Leonardo da Vinci
- **SN** Water
- **SL** Richard Nixon

506
- **G** A kangaroo
- **E** Klinger
- **H** Edward Heath
- **AL** Norman Rockwell
- **SN** Antibodies
- **SL** Richard Dunn

507
- **G** Exeter
- **E** *Tutti Fruitti*
- **H** Spencer Percival
- **AL** Four years
- **SN** Direct current
- **SL** Hockenheim

508
- **G** Alcoholics
- **E** Mary Pickford; her husband was Douglas Fairbanks
- **H** George Washington
- **AL** Turner
- **SN** A battery
- **SL** No

509
- **G** Indonesia's
- **E** Madonna
- **H** Hitler
- **AL** George IV
- **SN** Bile
- **SL** Rachel Heyhoe-Flint

510
- **G** Sierra Leone's
- **E** *From a Jack to a King*
- **H** Syphilis
- **AL** The Houses of Parliament
- **SN** Biodegradable
- **SL** Sir Gordon Richards

511
- **G** The USA
- **E** Humphrey Bogart and Lauren Bacall
- **H** Catherine of Aragon
- **AL** Regent Street
- **SN** Platelets
- **SL** Silver

512
- **G** Aber
- **E** 1989
- **H** Yes
- **AL** Casca
- **SN** Antelope
- **SL** Gary Lineker

513
- **G** China's
- **E** *McCloud*
- **H** Princess Michael of Kent's
- **AL** Enamel
- **SN** Lime
- **SL** Walking

514
- **G** Newfoundland
- **E** *The Great Dictator*
- **H** Spain and France
- **AL** La Scala
- **SN** Romeo
- **SL** Two

515
- **G** Nicaragua
- **E** *Singing In the Rain*
- **H** Paris
- **AL** Pianos weren't invented until the 18th century
- **SN** Corinth
- **SL** Shooting

516
- **G** Haiti's
- **E** Mickey Mouse's
- **H** Ceylon
- **AL** Neptune
- **SN** On its feathers
- **SL** Shrimps

517
- **G** Aberdeen
- **E** Metropolis
- **H** Ireland
- **AL** Avalon
- **SN** Bed-wetting
- **SL** The Princess Royal, Princess Anne

518
- **G** Switzerland
- **E** Gale
- **H** Warren Hastings
- **AL** Et cetera
- **SN** The ostrich
- **SL** The Sydney Cricket Ground

519
- **G** Zurich's
- **E** Mel Blanc
- **H** Calcutta
- **AL** 41
- **SN** A pup
- **SL** Three

520
- **G** The Appian Way
- **E** General Custer
- **H** Bonnie Prince Charlie
- **AL** The Beatles
- **SN** A bat
- **SL** Ten

521
- **G** Abergavenny
- **E** W.C. Fields's real name was William Claud Dunkenfield
- **H** 19th
- **AL** Ted Hughes
- **SN** A lever
- **SL** Gravy

522
- **G** Aberystwyth
- **E** A Tony
- **H** Yes
- **AL** Tchaikovsky's
- **SN** One sixteenth
- **SL** Three

523
- **G** Icebergs
- **E** *Desperately Seeking Susan*
- **H** Peter Phillips
- **AL** Pan (panpipes)
- **SN** An alkali
- **SL** The Grand National

524
- **G** Edinburgh
- **E** *Dune*
- **H** John F. Kennedy
- **AL** Bert Weedon
- **SN** Sir Isaac Newton
- **SL** W. G. Grace

525
- **G** French
- **E** Ukelele
- **H** The Beatle Cut
- **AL** The Thompson Twins
- **SN** Seven miles per second
- **SL** Baseball

526
- **G** Lyndon B. Johnson
- **E** Monks
- **H** The Desert Rats
- **AL** Customs Officer
- **SN** Marie Curie was Polish; she won her second Nobel Prize for Chemistry
- **SL** Baseball

527
- **G** Guatemala City
- **E** Val Doonican
- **H** Elizabeth I
- **AL** Beryl Cook
- **SN** Those cut in the afternoon
- **SL** A soccer ball

528
- **G** Caused mass destruction — Fifi was a hurricane
- **E** Mick Jagger
- **H** The Crusaders were children
- **AL** *As You Like It*
- **SN** Eleven
- **SL** Romania

529
- **G** Sugar
- **E** Lenny Henry and Ade Edmonson are the husbands of Dawn French and Jennifer Saunders
- **H** William McKinley
- **AL** Charles Kingsley
- **SN** Sleep
- **SL** Took a lift over part of the course

530
- **G** Belgium
- **E** *Stir Crazy*
- **H** All-day opening began on that day
- **AL** Manchester's
- **SN** Hybrid
- **SL** Weightlifting's

531
G Sri Lanka
E Joan Collins
H City Airport
AL *The Tempest*
SN The Greenhouse Effect
SL The hammer

532
G Hungarian
E The Who
H France
AL St. Paul's Cathedral
SN Two
SL First to fly non-stop around the world without refuelling

533
G Java
E *Suspicious Minds*
H Mexico
AL Westminster Cathedral
SN To use as a compass
SL Lewis

534
G Iraq
E George Harrison
H Thomas á Beckett
AL A pot of paint
SN Wind velocity
SL Lewis

535
G Iraq
E *Space Oddity*
H Shogun
AL The lips
SN The top row
SL Terry Marsh

536
G The Blue Mountains
E *Honky Tonk Woman*
H Genghis Khan
AL Bellini
SN To control snakes
SL Great Britain

537
G Easter Island's
E Nothing
H Nine
AL "Publish and be damned"
SN Quads
SL Great Britain

538
G "Land of the Rising Sun"
E Bessie Smith
H Thirteenth
AL The Tabard Inn, Southwark
SN 7th January
SL Manchester United

539
G Covent Garden
E No
H Killed himself
AL *The Time Machine*
SN Woofs
SL Martina Navratilova

540
G Ethiopia
E *The King of Rock 'n' Roll*
H Harry Houdini
AL Lord Byron of Rochdale
SN Elm
SL Her brother John

541
G The Tay
E The Fat Boys
H The Berlin Wall
AL Nixon
SN Three
SL Billie Jean King

542
G Three
E P-E-P-A
H Patrick Nicholl
AL *The Star Spangled Banner*
SN Average
SL Holland

543
G The Corinth Canal links the Aegean with the Ionian
E Fleetwood Mac
H Abraham Lincoln's body
AL Arnold Bennett
SN Drams
SL The Davis Cup

544
G Caernarvon Castle
E *Let It Be*
H Edward I
AL The Great Sham of Literature
SN Celluloid
SL Prince Charles

545
G Burma
E Ziggy Marley
H Princess Beatrice
AL 16th
SN Moth balls
SL *Octopussy*

546
G Disneyworld
E Yazz
H 1976
AL Andy Warhol designed the logo for the Rolling Stones
SN Chromium
SL Tarzan

547
G India's
E The Hollies
H Comet
AL Cells
SN A shellfish
SL Rugby

548
G Martin
E *Nathan Jones*
H Uniforms
AL The Pushmi-Pullyu
SN They turn white
SL None

549
G Brussels'
E *Sail Away*
H Louis XIV
AL Swiss Family Robinson
SN Pharmacophobia is the fear of drugs
SL Pakistan

550
G Flamingo
E Elvis Presley
H Corfe Castle
AL John Gay
SN He gave his name to the begonia
SL From the back

551
G Alderney
E The Bitter
H Henry II
AL Mr. Toad
SN The raccoon
SL Two

552
G Lunch
E "Oh my love, my darling"
H Zimbabwe's
AL No
SN Ants
SL Chick peas

553
G Canada's
E Bros
H Geoffrey Howe's
AL William Shakespeare
SN Milton Friedman
SL Greek

554
G Bristol
E Queen
H White
AL Captain Ahab
SN The rhinoceros
SL Seven no trumps

555
G The Pyrenees
E Status Quo's
H Spain
AL *The Pirates of Penzance*
SN The Kodiak bear
SL Sir Matt Busby

556
G Singapore's
E *The Little Mermaid*
H Margaret Thatcher
AL The left arm
SN Felt
SL East Germany

557
G Gloves
E *Telethon*
H 18
AL Mahler's
SN Ultra violet
SL W G Grace captained England at bowls

558
G A star and the moon
E Prefab Sprout
H German
AL *The Eroica*
SN Lyme Regis (accept Charmouth)
SL Seventeen

559
G Italy
E George Michael
H Edward VIII
AL Joan Sutherland
SN Graphite
SL Yahtzee

560
G Kathmandu
E The Rolling Stones
H Elizabeth I
AL Yellow
SN The brain
SL Lester Piggott

· O R D E R   F O R M ·

HOW TO ORDER YOUR BOXTREE QUIZ BOOKS

TV	242 8	15–1 QUIZ	£2.99
TV	135 9	15–1 SUPERCHALLENGE QUIZ	£2.99
TV	695 4	$64,000 QUESTION BOOK	£2.99
TV	298 3	CATCHPHRASE QUIZ	£2.99
	291 6	CORONATION STREET QUIZ	£2.99
TV	072 7	COUNTDOWN PUZZLE BOOK	£2.99
TV	694 6	CROSS WITS QUIZ	£2.99
TV	708 X	DICKIE DAVIS' SPORTS QUIZ	£2.99
TV	266 5	KRYPTON FACTOR QUIZ	£2.99
	729 2	MOVIE SUPERCHALLENGE QUIZ	£2.99
TV	735 7	STRIKE IT LUCKY QUIZ	£2.99
	028 X	SUPERSOAPS QUIZ NO.1	£2.99
	279 9	SUPERSOAPS QUIZ NO.2	£2.99
	604 0	SUPERSOAPS QUIZ NO.3	£2.99
	261 4	TV'S GREATEST HITS QUIZ	£2.99
	767 5	WILLIAM HILL HORSE RACING QUIZ	£2.99
TV	593 1	TRIVIAL PURSUIT – TV EDITION	£7.99

All these books are available at your local bookshop or newsagent, or can be ordered direct from the publisher. Just tick the titles you want and fill in the form below.

Prices and availability subject to change without notice.

Boxtree Cash Sales, P.O. Box 11, Falmouth, Cornwall TR10 9EN.

Please send cheque or postal order for the value of the book, and add the following for postage and packing:

U.K. including B.F.P.O. – £1.00 for one book, plus 50p for the second book, and 30p for each additional book ordered up to a £3.00 maximum.

Overseas including Eire – £2.00 for the first book, plus £1.00 for the second book, and 50p for each additional book ordered.

OR please debit this amount from my Access/Visa Card (delete as appropriate).

Card No. _____

Amount £ _____ Exp. Date _____

Signed _____

Name _____

Address _____

_____

_____